Decision Time

A Guide to
Career Enhancement

Third Edition

Michael Shahnasarian, Ph.D.

**Decision Time:
A Guide to Career Enhancement, Third Edition**
is a Publication of the
National Career Development Association.

i

————

Library of Congress Cataloging-in-Publication Data

Shahnasarian, Michael.
    Decision time : a guide to career enhancement / Michael Shahnasarian.
        p. cm.
    Includes bibliographical references.
    ISBN 1-885333-13-7
    1. Career changes. 2. Career development. I. Title.
    HF5384.S48 2005
    650.14--dc22

                                2005620110

Table of Contents

Foreword

An insightful and well-constructed plan is essential to accomplishing your objectives – whatever they may be. This is perhaps most true of decisions pertaining to your career development. Of all the decisions you encounter during your lifetime, career decisions are among the most important since they impact, among other things, how you apply your talents, your quality of life, and the fulfillment you realize from your daily labor.

Career decisions affect people from all walks of life and at various times during their lifetimes. Regardless of the level of education you choose to pursue, whether you embark on a military or civilian career path – or a combination – or the occupation, specialty, or industry your career path takes you down, you will encounter career decisions of various degrees of importance and complexity along the way. Questions about our careers confront us from childhood through retirement. It seems like there is always a career issue in our midst, and we feel compelled to make the "right" decision.

The third edition of *Decision Time: A Guide to Career Enhancement* can help you to focus your career objectives, gain important information, make quality career decisions, form a sound career planning strategy, and manage your career development to help you to realize your objectives. I recommend that you invest time in the book's recommended activities, and use it to guide your career progress.

Decision Time's professional guidance and exercises will help you to navigate through the myriad of career-related decisions that have prompted you to use it – both now and in the future. Its format is inviting, thought provoking, and practical.

In an increasingly complex, technologically sophisticated world that is, paradoxically, becoming smaller and more integrated every day, anything less than a well-managed and planned approach to career decision making and planning places you at risk of not realizing your objectives. You have my best wishes in your career development.

H. Norman Schwarzkopf
General, U.S. Army, Retired

Testimonials

"Distilled wisdom from 20 years of career counseling practice, this strategic roadmap offers hope and direction while inspiring readers to see the connection among career management, well-being and fulfillment!"
— Rich Feller, Ph.D., Professor,
Counseling and Career Development, Colorado State University

"Updated for today's job hunters, the classic *Decision Time* offers solid practical advice for the 21st century workplace. The tone is friendly; the content is professional; the exercises, motivational stories, and examples are engaging; and the hands-on activities are carefully described and placed clearly in the context of career management. I would recommend it without hesitation."
— Jane Goodman Ph.D., NCC, NCCC, Professor, Counseling, Oakland University
Past President of American Counseling Association and
National Career Development Association

"A very thorough, self-help book that college students or any job seeker needs to understand the process of career planning and how to complete its steps. The book gives extensive information about how to assess one's self and then relate that information to the job market, while always advocating that one's career choices are central to life meaning. The book offers many worksheets and activities that can help a serious career explorer to either choose the first occupation or to make career transitions."
— JoAnn Harris-Bowlsbey, Ed.D., Career Development Leadership Alliance
Past President, National Career Development Association

"This excellent highly-practical guide offers the reader all the necessary tools to competently navigate through a systematic lifestyle/career evaluation or adjustment process. The reader-friendly, straight forward style of the workbook, coupled with the well-constructed counseling instruments, career management tips, decision-making advice, consumer information, printed references and Web sites will immeasurably aid both individuals who would like to examine their own life/career path and counselors to assess their clients' personal and career options. In brief, Dr. Shahnasarian's latest contribution to clients and practitioners will be a smashing success that will be a sparkling jewel among the many wonderful publications of NCDA."
— Frank Karpati, MA, LPC, NCC, NCCC, NCSC, NCGC, Fellow – NCDA
Career Directions, Executive Director
Clifton Public Schools, Counselor

"Authoritative. Even definitive. Dr. Shahnasarian has proven himself to be the most experienced and respected career counselor of our time. Career decisions matter now more than ever in terms of your quality of life, so forget the quick fix. Why not take the time you need and follow a proven method. In Decision Time, it's all here: preparation, decision making, commitment and execution. Whether you are careering or re-careering, this is must reading and you may expect the best. You won't be disappointed."

— Brian T. McMahon, Ph.D., CRC
Professor, Virginia Commonwealth University, Dept. of Rehabilitation Counseling
Research Professor, VCU Dept. of Rehab Medicine

"An excellent resource for those in need of managing their careers effectively. Mike's approach provides a sensitive understanding of the difficulties people can encounter in their careers while also offering strategies for moving forward. Moreover, career counselors will find this book to be an excellent resource as they search for effective interventions to incorporate into their work with clients."

— Spencer G. Niles, Ph.D., Professor of Education, Penn State University
Past President, National Career Development Association

"An important book for anyone who is approaching a career decision. The book recommends a career decision process that is to be used throughout a person's life. Mike clearly knows that career planning requires ongoing evaluating and adjustments. This book will take much of the anxiety out of making career decisions."

— Mark Pope, Ed.D., NCC, MCC, MAC, ACS
Immediate Past President, American Counseling Association (2004-2005)
Associate Professor, University of Missouri— St. Louis

"An outstanding and easy-to-read guide to the often stressful job search process . . . practical and focused techniques . . . a tool that every job seeker and career counselor should have in their library."

— David M. Reile, Ph.D., Career Counselor and Organizational Consultant
Career Development Leadership Alliance

"Dr. Shahnasarian's knowledge of career development, human behavior, and life-long learning makes *Decision Time: A Guide to Career Enhancement, 3rd Edition* a must for job seekers. It provides the needed tools for taking charge of one's career with competence, confidence, and passion."

— Nancy K. Schlossberg, Ed. D, Professor Emerita, University of Maryland
Past President, National Career Development Association

"Career decisions are among the most important decisions an individual can make. Dr. Shahnasarian is a highly respected private practice career counselor and organizational consultant who has managed to translate his many years of experience and expertise into a highly readable book about how to make good quality career decisions. *Decision Time* is research based and offers practical strategies and suggestions. It provides activities to help determine work values, illustrates how interests can be translated into career options, and even provides step-by-step guidelines for conducting an effective job search. I would recommend *Decision Time: A Guide to Career Enhancement, 3rd Edition* to anyone – students, individuals in transition, and even career counselors for use with their clients."

— R. Bob Smith, III, Ph.D.
Chairman and CEO, Psychological Assessment Resources, Inc. (PAR)
Odessa, Florida

"For those unemployed and the one-in-three workers who are either dissatisfied with and/or convinced they are powerless over their work situation, *Decision Time* is the answer. Author and career development expert, Michael Shahnasarian, Ph.D., outlines an effective process for lifetime career management. The book deftly guides prospective career-changers through a process that emphasizes the how-to of effective career decision-making. Career counselors will find chapter-end discussion questions and "Take Action" implementation activities useful as in-session or as "homework" exercises for individual or group (e.g., job-search club) counseling. Job seekers will be compelled by the pragmatic, sequential decision-making approach. The book is perfect for adults searching for career-life satisfaction."

— Michael Hall, Ph.D., CMF, Private Practice Career Counselor
Charlotte, North Carolina

"*Decision Time* is a comprehensive, easy-to-use tool for anyone contemplating a career change or making a career decision. The six-step approach is logical and clear: each step in the sequence is treated thoroughly and in an engaging manner, while the steps themselves flow seamlessly through the decision process. Moreover, the learning activities at each step illuminate important lessons in career decision-making. Finally, the appendices, with references and linkages to high-quality career resources, are extremely valuable in their own right. Indeed, Dr. Shahnasarian's book will be used over and over again."

— Gary W. Peterson, Ph.D.
Professor and Director of Training, Psychological Services in Education
Florida State University

To Mom

About the Author

Michael Shahnasarian, Ph.D., is the founder and president of Career Consultants of America, Inc., in Tampa, Florida. His practice specializes in career development, human resources consultation, life care planning, and vocational rehabilitation. Additionally, Dr. Shahnasarian has consulted and testified as an expert witness on vocational issues throughout the United States and abroad.

Dr. Shahnasarian earned a doctorate in counseling psychology at Florida State University, a master's degree in psychology at Texas A&M University, and a bachelor's degree in psychology at Indiana University. His specialty credentials include licensing as both a psychologist and mental health counselor, and board certifications as a career counselor, vocational evaluator, rehabilitation counselor, and life care planner. He has published five books and more than 40 articles on career development topics in various professional and industry publications.

PricewaterhouseCoopers recognized Dr. Shahnasarian as Up and Comer of the Year in 1988. Dr. Shahnasarian was selected 1989 Human Resource Professional of the Year by the American Society for Training and Development. He was the 1990 recipient of the Outstanding Alumni Award for Business and Industry presented by Florida State University. The Florida Career Development Association recognized Dr. Shahnasarian as Business and Industry Professional of the Year in 1992. In 1995, the Department of Psychology at Texas A&M University selected Dr. Shahnasarian Outstanding Graduate in psychology for the first 25 years of the department's history. Dr. Shahnasarian was selected for a 1996 merit award presented by the National Career Development Association. The American Rehabilitation Counselor Association selected Dr. Shahnasarian as Rehabilitation Counselor of the Year in 1999, and the National Career Development Association presented the Outstanding Career Practitioner Award to him in 2002. He was named a Fellow of the National Career Development Association in 2002.

Leadership in professional and civic organizations has also been a feature of Dr. Shahnasarian's career development. He served as 1998 president of the National Career Development Association. Former Florida Governor Lawton Chiles appointed Dr. Shahnasarian to the Florida Rehabilitation Council in 1998; Governor Jeb Bush reappointed him in 2000. From 1998 through 2003, Dr. Shahnasarian served as a columnist for the *USA Today* Web site, responding to career-related questions readers posed. Dr. Shahnasarian currently serves on the editorial boards of three professional publications: *Career Development Quarterly, Rehabilitation Professional, and Journal of Applied Rehabilitation Counseling.*

Preface

The first edition of *Decision Time: A Guide to Career Enhancement* was expanded from an earlier workbook I wrote in 1986, *Making Career Decisions*. Psychological Assessment Resources (PAR) published the first edition of *Decision Time* in 1994, and the second edition was subsequently translated in Italian under the title *Il Lavoro Per Me* and published by Organizzazioni Speciali in 2003. The National Career Development (NCDA), a professional organization representing thousands of career counselors worldwide, invited this updated, third edition of *Decision Time*.

Since its initial publication more than a decade ago, thousands of diverse individuals across the globe have used *Decision Time* to guide their career decision making and planning. *Decision Time* has been used in many formats. Some have worked through it alone, while others have used it under a career counselor's guidance. The book has also been used in career planning classes offered at colleges and universities, and many business and government organizations have included *Decision Time* in employee mentoring and succession planning programs.

The first, second, and third editions of *Decision Time* have the same aim: to offer those wanting guidance in their career decision making and planning a sound method, based on career development theory and research, encompassed in a practical and efficient intervention. To this end, a career decision-making model – emanating from the work of Frank Parsons in 1909 and refined over the years by the likes of Donald Super, John Holland, and John Krumboltz – serves as the core of both editions.

Career development professionals will recognize the integration and melding of the profession's central theoretical bases – including trait-factor, developmental self-concept, personality, and behavioral. The book is not intended to be a textbook. In keeping with its aim, however, I hope readers find *Decision Time* easy to use, empowering and, above all, helpful in making important life and career decisions, as well as in planning how to implement them.

The passing of time and my appreciation of the many changes since the first edition's publication, my experience using *Decision Time*, and comments from colleagues, clients, and other readers have allowed me to evaluate the first edition's merits and to assess how to improve it. Resources like *Decision Time* are similar to careers: both require ongoing assessment, analysis, and refinement to ensure progress toward established objectives. The opportunity to improve upon the first edition and update *Decision Time* so it could optimally benefit individuals seeking career guidance today motivated me to write this third edition.

Like its predecessors, the assumptions underlying this edition of *Decision Time* are twofold. My first assumption is that those who choose to read and use this book view work as central to their well being, self-fulfillment, and even to their identities. That is, they view work as much more than a means to earn a living, and they are unwilling to settle for a job that does not promise an opportunity to further their personal and career goals.

In our society, work has become almost a defining feature of our existence. How often have you gone to a social gathering – or other type of gathering, for that matter – when someone very early in the conversation asks the standard, introductory cliché, "So, what do you do?" From this very brief interaction, people often form long-lasting impressions about us.

Of course, while one very basic reason most of us work is to provide the means to meet our financial commitments, work provides far more than a way to subsist. If you derive little else than financial reward from your work, you are missing out on a big part of your self-fulfillment.

When you think about it, we spend an overwhelming portion of our lives either preparing for the workplace or working. Consider that the average person sleeps 8 hours per day; that leaves 16 hours for other activities. From the time we are roughly 5 years old through the time we retire in our 60s or beyond, most of us are involved in vocational activities – educational and work – one-half or more of those remaining hours, 5 days per week. If you are unfulfilled in your work life, your dissatisfaction will most certainly affect other areas of your life: namely, your self-esteem, relationships with those close to you, your lifestyle, and your work performance.

We gain a great deal from a healthy work situation and positive career development – starting with a healthy self-esteem. People who do not feel good about what they do, feel their work has little importance or value, or who have negative feelings about their employer or work situation usually do not feel good about themselves.

When you think about it, many of our acquaintances and social relationships also develop through the workplace. It makes sense that if you spend half your waking hours during most of your adult life at work, many of your social interactions will come through those you meet through your job.

A troublesome work situation can also spawn a wide range of physical problems. Perhaps you have experienced some of these: headaches, stress-related disorders, sleep problems, ulcers, and substance abuse are just a few physical problems that a negative work situation can provoke.

Above all, however, work gives us dignity and purpose. Accomplishing something others value is one of the greatest satisfactions we can realize; work gives us an opportunity to make this happen.

The second assumption inherent in *Decision Time* relates to the commitment and energy necessary to truly manage and take control of your career development. Our workplace grows more complex every day. To develop a fulfilling career that allows you to come close to realizing your career potential requires that you invest in quality career decision making and planning. Even after you have focused your career goals, you must develop a sound strategy and a determined will to keep on track.

In the not-too-distant past, people commonly spent most of their careers with one or two employers. Perhaps this type of career history is true of your parents or relatives. For better or worse, this is no longer the case.

Experts on career decision making encounter many individuals who change occupations multiple times during their lifetimes. I have found that quite often these changes are major. I recall one client who was a medical doctor on the faculty at a medical school; he decided to return to school at age 48 to train for employment as a tanker captain.

Sometimes a career change is self-initiated – prompted by the economy, a physical or mental health condition, or changes at one's place of employment. With a global economy changing by the day – fast-changing philosophies about how to structure and operate corporations, rapid changes brought by new technologies, and sometimes uncontrollable organizational dynamics that involve mergers, acquisitions, and downsizings – the workplace of tomorrow will become even more complex. Well-managed career development will be vital to success.

Decision Time presumes that you can take control of your career – even in a complex, unpredictable labor market – and realize your career goals. This requires hard work, a well-planned and executed strategy, and ongoing career management.

Decision Time uses a model to help you structure your approach to career decision making and planning – an overwhelming task for anyone, whatever your background. Also included are structured activities to help you explore your most important work values, examine how your interests translate to career options that may be unfamiliar to you, examine your strengths, and help you reflect on personal issues concerning your career.

After you have pondered your career decision from a personal perspective, *Decision Time* presents proven techniques to help you cut through the red tape and secure accurate, up-to-date, and complete career information so you can effectively evaluate your career options. Suggestions on how to research the most pertinent information that will help you better understand your options are presented.

Many people have difficulty moving beyond the research phase and into the commitment phase of career decision making. *Decision Time* presents guidance to help you make a quality career decision and plan a strategy best suited for you.

Most people conduct multiple job searches during their careers, and I have found that many readers of *Decision Time* begin searching for a job during their use of the book. For this reason, I have included a discussion of what I have found to be essential practices among those who get the job they want – *quickly!* Finally, *Decision Time* offers in-depth suggestions for developing your career strategy.

Your work in *Decision Time* will assist you not only with your pending career decision, it will help you make career decisions that you will invariably face throughout your life and career development. Perhaps most important in your use of this book will be learning a method to guide you in making quality career decisions and formulating personal career-development strategies. No one is going to do it for you. Unless you take responsibility for your career direction, you will likely find yourself less than fully satisfied with your career development.

Use of *Decision Time* with added counsel from a trained career development professional – such as a career counselor or career development facilitator – can enhance your experience. Many career development professionals have found *Decision Time* useful as homework between counseling sessions.

Special thanks to Todd A. Wilber, who provided technical writing assistance, and to Robert C. Reardon, who encouraged this third edition and provided guidance in its evolution.

Why Do People See a Career Counselor?

Shortly after I meet with a person for career counseling I ask, "What brought you here today to talk to a career counselor?" Some of the responses I have heard follow; many, I am sure, will be responses with which you may identify.

I think I'm experiencing burnout and have been for a while. What brought me here is a desire to make a change.

I'm tired of teaching. I want to do something else.

The number one reason I'm here is that I made a New Year's resolution to put my career on track. It was severely derailed last year. I want to have total control over my next job change. I want to have a planned approach and focus.

I just need some direction and thought.

I feel like I've been in a rut. I want to advance the practical skills I have. I like the service industry.

I have worked practically all of my life. I quit when my husband became ill; he died earlier this year. Now it's time to move on.

My job is boring – not challenging.

I've been in college off and on for so long with very little idea of what it is I'm doing and why I'm there. I'm just kind of drifting. I think it's time to zero in on something.

I've been in banking 21 years. I'm no longer interested in it. It's run its course.

I'm going to reenter the workforce. I'm almost through with a divorce and I want to move forward. I thought this would be a good time to reevaluate where I'm going.

I want to gain some foothold – expertise – on how to find a new career.

I'm interested in a career change.

I'm very unhappy with what I'm doing – I'm always worrying about what's going on at work. I don't feel my job is secure.

I feel in some ways like I never found my niche.

I feel like I'm basically deadlocked in my job – not getting anywhere in terms of promotion or pay raises.

Everyone is pressuring me to go to college; I'm not sure that's right for me – at least at this time. I'm just really fascinated with sea life.

I don't know what I want to do.

I went into the military because I had no idea of what I wanted to do. Now I'm out and I still don't know what I want to do.

I was laid off from my job last Tuesday. I thought this might give me new ideas.

I feel like I'm at a dead end. Every day [at work] it's the same thing over and over.

I have decided to leave the practice of law. I was mismatched for my profession.

My company is consolidating its offices. I have to decide whether I want to stay with them and accept the transfer.

I need a systematic approach [to career decision making] rather than trial-and-error.

My situation has led me to conclude that I'm in a self-confidence crisis. I feel unsure about what to do and where to go.

I'm stuck. I'm trying to refocus for the third time in my life.

I'm really not happy doing what I'm doing. Before I just leap into something I want to make sure I've carefully analyzed it. I don't want to change direction and find out I'm not any closer [to career satisfaction] than I was before.

I feel totally helpless. I have no idea how people get a job. I feel so naive.

I'm not making enough money.

I'm trying to get some help with networking – tapping into the hidden job market. Right now I feel a little unfocused.

As you can see, I've done lots of things. I've been needing some career direction.

Just because at this point it's the first time I have an opportunity to make my own choice instead of just doing what my father wants me to do.

I need to decide what to do the rest of my life.

I'm totally dissatisfied with my work. I have some strong skills that the system won't allow me to use.

I'm bored with my job. I don't have any interest in it and [I] just dread going to work.

I have many ideas about what I'd like to do. I'd like someone to give me some guidelines.

I feel I've got to make a change. I'm not sure the business world is for me.

I was mad about my last performance review. I want to make sure that I'm in the right career.

A drunk driver slammed into my car and now I have physical limits to what I can do. I need to make a career change.

I want to be in a position where I have more control over my time and my work.

Chapter 1

✧

Career Decision Making:
A Lifelong Process

"The Question"

For many people, career decisions are among their most recurrent and problematic decisions. The question, "What do you want to be when you grow up?" confronts us early, and vestiges of it sometimes haunt us into adolescence, early adulthood, and beyond. We sometimes hear "the question" aloud, directed by those familiar and those scarcely known to us. At other times, it emanates from our psyche.

"What do you want to be when you grow up?" is a question that evokes a range of emotions and responses. It can intimidate or motivate us, embarrass us or evoke pride. Sometimes it causes us to behave defensively or boastfully. Whatever our response, "the question" is usually provocative and occasionally touches a nerve.

Variations of "What do you want to be when you grow up?" include "When are you going to start making a decent living?", "How long are you going to continue in a job in which you are unhappy and underachieving your potential?", "When are you going to settle down and find a real job?", and "Are your claimed problems really so severe that they cause you not to progress with your career development?" Again, these questions are sometimes stated explicitly; at other times, they are veiled or come from our unconscious.

Focusing on "the question" provokes insight on how these simple 10 words can affect us so profoundly. Consider the following points:

- The "what," as in *"What* do you want to be . . ."* implies that the individual to whom the question is directed has a choice. This is not always the case, and sometimes discerning available career options is overwhelming.

- Because "the question" incorporates a future component, it connotes that career potential has yet to be fully harnessed or converted, which can be unsettling to those less than satisfied with their career progress.

- Depending on the circumstances in which "the question" is presented, it can imply that the intended respondent is somehow deficient because his or her career objectives are not apparent, or artifacts of career success (e.g., goal-directed activities, impressive job title, material possessions) are not readily evident.

- Failing to have a stellar answer to "What do you want to be when you grow up?" is, to many, an admission of weaknesses that include indecisiveness and lack of focus. After all, our society values those with vision and self-assuredness. Anything less than a direct, well-outlined response, many feel will cause them to be judged askance by the individual who posed the question – interestingly, someone who often asks "the question" from a position of personal career turmoil. Being labeled as an underachiever – whether self-imposed or by others – is an anathema few want.

- Since we usually first hear "the question" when we are children and then repeatedly through youth and adulthood, it often conjures memories of career objectives we previously held. To many, memories of prior career happenings that have been less successful than hoped evoke distress.

- The " . . . when you grow up?" part of "the question" can suggest that you are in a less than mature state – something that can instinctively trigger a defensive reaction.

- There is no end point to one's career development, as implied in the words "to be" that appear in "What do you want *to be* . . ." The workplace in which our career develops is dynamic, as are our personal situations, career interests, and work values. That is, career decision making and planning is a lifelong process rather than a discrete event.

Many wrestle with "the question" or variations of it throughout their career development. I have found that among those most preoccupied with "the question" are people you would least suspect – those who appear focused, accomplished, and satisfied. I have also found that it is not a matter of chance that the status of their career development appears in good order. Their preoccupation with "the question," appreciation of its complexities, and the skills they have developed to make prudent career decisions and associated career plans often enable them to make the most out of their options.

Career decisions and "the question" in its various forms confront us throughout our career development and sometimes recur when we least expect. Choosing a high school curriculum . . . determining whether to pursue a trade, college, or enter the job market . . . selecting a college major . . . deciding whether to apply for a job or promotion . . . contemplating whether developing new skills through retraining is in order . . . assessing the feasibility of self-employment . . . evaluating career satisfaction during mid-career or another point . . . opting for a career change . . . reassessing career options after experiencing a layoff or downsizing . . . reentering the world of work after a major personal event such as a divorce and absence from the workplace, or after acquiring disabling problems . . . wrestling with retirement . . . and even feeling disappointment with retirement and contemplating a return to work . . . these are but a few events we encounter over our life span that prompt career decision making.

At times, others have forewarned us of the career decisions we confront. At other times, career dilemmas occur unexpectedly.

Career Decision Making and Life Satisfaction

Of course, career decisions are constantly encountered during our lives. The consequences of poor or less than optimal decisions can include strain in relationships, financial hardship, dissatisfaction with both self and work, and psychological maladjustment.

Some experts estimate that half of our waking hours for up to two-thirds of our lives (between the time we enter school and the time we leave the workplace) are consumed with work-related activities – namely, education/training, and employment. After all, most of us prepare for or sleep up to one third – 8 hours – of the day. During 8 of the remaining 16 hours, we typically pursue career-related activities. This does not include the time we spend in activities such as working overtime, preparing for work, or traveling to and from work.

Simply put, work and its related activities consume a major portion of our life. Given how much time we spend in these activities and the impact of our career development on our existence – including our self-esteem, financial well being, and lifestyle – common sense dictates that being less than satisfied with your career development can compromise your life satisfaction.

Despite the strong correlation between career fulfillment and life satisfaction, few people attempt to manage their careers. Many adopt a reactive rather than a proactive approach. That is, rather than establishing clear objectives, creating and seeking opportunities that promise to further goals, and pursuing, evaluating, and developing career opportunities in concert with preestablished objectives, they passively react to situations they encounter.

A reactive approach to career development invites submission and subordination of personal objectives. Examples include waiting for events to impact you rather than attempting to mold events; relinquishing control of your career to the likes of family members, supervisors, or business partners – despite how well intentioned they may be; and making decisions about your career after experiencing negative events such as downsizing, pay cut, or demotion. Of course, these latter events are sometimes unavoidable. My point is, however, that the state of your career development is more likely to be in an advantaged position if you have invested quality effort in career decision making and planning, rather than reacting from a damage control perspective – especially when unforeseen and uncontrollable setbacks occur.

Career management involves a proactive approach that includes reflection, analysis, systematic decision making and planning, and purposeful activity. The concept assumes you can enhance your chances for career success and, correspondingly, life satisfaction. It requires discipline, perseverance, calculated risk taking, and ongoing reassessment and refinement of previously established objectives and plans.

Curiously, many people spend more time planning their annual vacations than planning and managing their career development. Many neglect tending to the status of their careers. They sometimes get comfortable in a job, though they are less than content with it. As time passes they often become more complacent and rationalize: "It's not that bad," "A job's a job," and "I don't want to start all over again." More time passes, and they become even less inclined to change jobs after realizing pay increases, employee benefits, and personal considerations – such as financial and family obligations – that further distract focus from their career dissatisfaction. Later, they may feel trapped in their less than satisfied career state: they second guess the value of their skills in the workplace, they doubt their ability to negotiate a transition to a more positive state of career development successfully and, sadly, they passively accept their fate. These people often view their jobs as "work" in a negative sense, synonymous with labor, toil, and lack of choice, all mutually exclusive of the positive connotations of the word – an activity that allows one to realize personal fulfillment.

As a career counselor, I have often thought of how unfortunate it is that so many people passively accept career dissatisfaction. Not liking your employer, supervisor, or coworkers; feeling unchallenged or unappreciated in your job; disliking the activities you undertake from day to day; looking ahead with dread to going to work – these are symptoms of career dissatisfaction. If you do not feel good about your job, it will quite likely aversely affect your personal life.

I am not advocating that going to work should be the highlight of your day or the center of your being – although I have met many people for whom this is true; some appear well adjusted, others do not. Few people lying in their death bed are likely to include among their last thoughts, "I wish I spent more time at work." What I am encouraging you to do, however, is to objectively review your career development to date, assess your satisfaction with it, and develop a plan to help guide you in a direction compatible with your desires.

Effective career decision making and planning skills are among the most important life survival skills you can develop. These skills can dictate how well you live and how happy you are with your life. Success in your career is not purely a matter of being gifted intellectually, being in the right place at the right time, or even being born into circumstances where attractive career options are available with little effort on your part. More often than not, those who realize their potential and enjoy fulfilling careers have done so through means well beyond raw talent and chance.

A career management philosophy includes establishing firm objectives and purposefully initiating activities that promise to bring predetermined objectives to fruition. Assessing presenting opportunities, honing skills necessary to enhance competitiveness, and strategically approaching and developing sought-out opportunities are among the tactics those who manage their career development employ. Inherent in this approach is forethought, intent, and purpose.

A motivational speaker I once heard conveyed a strong message about the importance of career management through a theater analogy. In contrast to actors who play assigned roles and have opportunities for dress rehearsals, repeat performances, and parts in other productions, career development in the contemporary workplace does not offer opportunities of this sort. We have but one career – without opportunities to practice or to do it over. Your career development deserves careful attention.

Before you go to the next chapter, I recommend that you ponder the following questions:

1. Have you recently encountered the question, "What do you want to be when you grow up?" either directly or in an alternate form? If so, how was it presented? What reaction did "the question" evoke in you? Why do you believe "the question" was posed to you?

2. Looking back at your career, have you adopted a proactive or reactive approach to your career development? Cite examples.

3. What ideas do you have for better managing your career development?

Chapter 2

⚜

Making Career Decisions:
A Step-by-Step Model

Overview

Professional career counselors have been providing guidance to help people optimize their decision making since 1905. Frank Parsons, considered the father of the modern career development profession, is credited with developing one of the first systematic vocational guidance methods. He practiced in Boston during the early twentieth century – a time when masses of immigrants were arriving in the United States, the country was transitioning from a largely agrarian economy, and efficiently integrating workers into a society burgeoning in the industrial revolution was critical. Over the years, the work place has become more sophisticated, new technologies have influenced how work is performed, social and political forces have complicated people's lives, and career counselors have continued to refine methods to guide decision making. Figure 1 presents a synopsis of selected social, political, and economic events that affected the workplace during the last century.

Work place change – along with associated implications confronting workers via more frequent, unpredictable, and complex decision making – is, perhaps, more prevalent than anytime in the history of humankind. Technological change and global developments occur rapidly and unpredictably, affecting the workplace in unanticipated ways. Consider, for example, the impact on millions of workers worldwide because of the end of the Cold War at the close of the last century, and the events of September 11, 2001, shortly after the dawn of this century. Those employed in defense, transportation, financial services, and security industries, to name a few, were affected in previously unimaginable ways.

Myriads of technological, economic, social, and political influences – such as Asian, Hispanic, and other foreign workers entering the American workplace in numbers reminiscent of Frank Parsons' day, while many American jobs are, simultaneously, being exported – are affecting untold numbers of people worldwide. The implications of the likes of stem cell research and developments in cyber technology have implications for future workplace change beyond our present comprehension. Here are a few other statistics to ponder when considering how unforeseen events may affect your career development.

- The percentage of working Americans over the age of 50 will increase to 38.3% by the year 2010. Experts attribute this to, among other things, the aging of the baby boom generation and improved health care, which contributes to a need for more financial resources to support a longer life span and to better physical conditioning to remain active in the work place. More individuals will be working longer into their lifetimes than ever before.

- Almost 4 million American workers suffered disabling injuries in 2000. Often these injuries impair ability to perform previous jobs, thus necessitating a career change. Severity of disability, transferability of previously established skill sets, phase of career development, and motivation to pursue vocational rehabilitation are among the factors that affect injured workers' capacity to make a positive transition.

- In a publication entitled *Working in the 21st Century,* the U.S. Department of Labor reports several workplace trends that include workers having shorter tenures with employers, more temporary workers being utilized, fewer new workers joining the labor force, and a higher percentage of older workers. The days of selecting a lifelong trade and then pursuing a job with one or two employers until retirement appears an artifact of bygone generations.

Figure 1. Selected Milestones in the Evolution of Career Development Practices in the Twentieth Century

1901–1920
Significant questions about the focus of education; World War I; expansion of vocational education; rising concern for mental hygiene.

1921–1940
Concern about the dignity and rights of children; psychological testing flourished; economic depression caused concern about job placement and unemployment; technological unemployment and worldwide depression were major social issues.

1941–1950
World War II; women entered the workforce in unprecedented numbers; higher education expanded to absorb veterans; postwar economic and industrial expansion; Cold War began with the Soviet Union.

1951–1960
Korean War; Sputnik launched, causing widespread debates about American education; education and guidance viewed as instruments of national defense.

1961–1970
Civil rights movement escalated; war in Vietnam caused major values upheavals and economic difficulties; major federal legislative outpouring to counteract unemployment, poverty, and other social ills; "Do your own thing" became a credo; rise in professionalism; computer-assisted career guidance-systems begin to emerge as important complements to career guidance and career counseling.

1971–1980
International tensions rose; energy problems emerged; unemployment, particularly of youth, became a major issue; concerns about overeducation and a lack of technical education emerged.

1981–2000
Many political changes swept the world: the Cold War ended; apartheid ended in South Africa; many nations formerly under communism moved to market economies; the global economy became a reality; the practice of career development became a worldwide phenomenon; women and minorities became major sources of new entrants to the workforce.

Note: Figure 1 is adapted from an article published by Edwin L. Herr and Michael Shahnasarian in the Special Millennium Issue of the *Career Development Quarterly* (March 2001). The figure is reprinted with permission from the National Career Development Association.

Clearly, many external conditions affect our career development and are beyond our control. Even some personal conditions – such as our health, family situations, and available resources – can be dictated to us with little or none of our influence.

Understandably, we sometimes feel we cannot control our career destiny. Few people have stumbled their ways to career success despite their strong abilities, great charm, or even after wonderful opportunities have been handed to them. Those who "get lucky" will likely be even fewer in the years ahead, considering the evolving complexities of the work place.

Those who thrive in their career development typically have navigated their career paths through effective decision making and planning. They tend to believe that their career and personal fulfillment are too precious to trust to fate, and they assume control, regardless of external and personal factors that may be impinging upon them. In effect, they learn to manage their career development and guide it in a direction they desire through activities that include:

- Introspection to determine personal requirements for career satisfaction.
- Researching opportunities and related information.

- Discerning and developing career options.
- When necessary, broadening and honing existing skills, as well as developing new skills.
- Employing sound strategies when making career decisions.
- Developing solid career plans.
- Remaining focused and disciplined.
- Selecting and applying appropriate "careering" activities.
- Evaluating progress and refining career plans as necessary.

This edition of *Decision Time: A Guide to Career Enhancement* will help you negotiate the activities listed above. The book aims to enhance your skills in career decision making and planning, thereby improving your opportunities to realize greater career fulfillment. Considering the relationship between career and life satisfaction, and the complex, recurrent nature of change everywhere in the workplace and certain to continue to confront you, these skills are among the most important you can develop.

A Proposed Model to Guide Your Career Decision Making

As a private practice career counselor, I often experience the uncomfortable feeling that some clients are relying too heavily on me to help them solve their career problems. Many have misconceptions about resources career counselors use. For example, surprising numbers of people call my office requesting to take "The Test," which they have heard "will tell me what I should be." Others, I sometimes feel, bestow a great deal of power in me – almost as if I had a crystal ball that I could look into and, after a session or two, unveil the perfect solution to their career problems.

Life offers no quick fix, short cut, or magic resource to solve career problems, make quality career decisions, or develop plans that implementing those decisions invariably require. Further, the answers to the very personal career decisions and issues you face are within you; beware of anyone who tells you anything different.

Sure, vocational tests can be very helpful in clarifying aspects about yourself that may not be apparent to you, and effective career counseling can facilitate your self-understanding and help you better explore your options. But the real answers to your career decisions remain within you. Finding the best answers requires a willingness to undergo honest reflection, painstaking research, and candor when committing to a decision.

Since Frank Parsons' pioneering efforts a century ago, career counselors have advocated a systematic approach to help people find answers while making career decisions. In the first edition of *Decision Time: A Guide to Career Enhancement*, I recommended a 5-step decision-making model; I am reintroducing the model in this edition. It underlies the process we will observe while addressing the career issues that are motivating you to invest in this book. The model appears in Figure 2 and is described in more detail in the following sections.

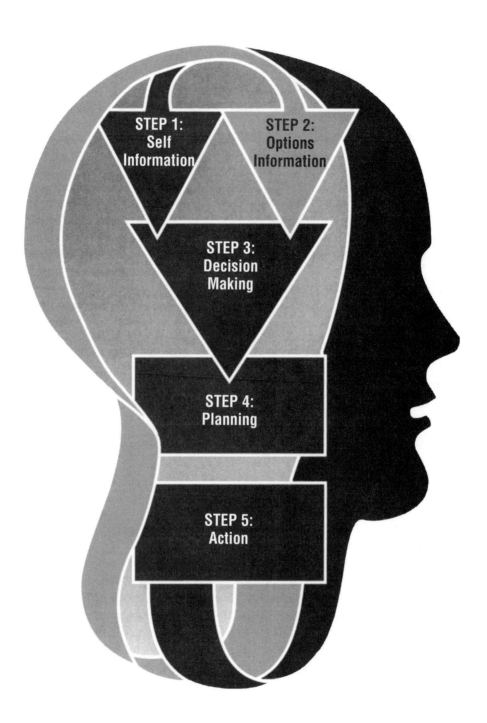

Figure 2. A model for decision making

Note. This figure appeared in the first edition of *Decision Time: A Guide to Career Enhancement*, which was published by Psychological Assessment Resources, Inc., in 1994. Michael Shahnasarian, Ph.D., has since acquired the rights to this work, and he consents to the figure's reproduction.

Step 1: Looking Within Yourself

As I suggested above, you must first look within yourself before you can truly understand and assess the potential for fulfillment your options promise. Too many people violate this basic principle of career decision making.

When career dissatisfaction rises to a level that prompts a desire for change, most people instinctively react by referring to sources such as the want ads in their Sunday newspapers, Internet job banks, and company Web sites. They may identify a few jobs that are somewhat appealing and on target with their background, and they then (a) half-heartedly send out a few resumes, (b) sigh heavily and complain about how poor the job market is, or (c) justify their procrastination in changing careers by telling themselves, "Well, maybe my job's not so bad after all." This constricted approach to career development will almost certainly inhibit your true career potential and lead to compromised career fulfillment.

You can begin to take control of your career development by taking time to look within yourself and discover, perhaps for the first time, what really is most important to you and to your career. Career counselors recommend that you focus your self-exploration in four areas:

- Work values
- Interests
- Skills
- Personal factors

I recommend that you begin your self-exploration by focusing on your work values. Needless to say, people have different perspectives on what they value or perceive as desirable. Some value high earnings, prestige, and opportunities for advancement. Others hold work values that include job security, good benefits, and a relatively stress-free work environment.

While there are no right or wrong work values, it is essential that you clearly identify what motivates you and what you find desirable if you are to seek and secure options, successfully, that are compatible with your set of values. We all have different priorities, and it is important that your chosen career path allows you the opportunity to satisfy your career needs. Identifying and understanding your priorities allows you to evaluate how well available options possibly match your needs.

Next, look within yourself to learn where your greatest interests lie. What is it that holds your attention for hours at a time and makes your heart race? What type of things do you find yourself daydreaming about? The challenge is to find career options that allow you the chance to have your interests satisfied.

A good quality career decision also requires you to critically evaluate your strengths and weaknesses, and to determine the types of aptitudes you wish to develop further. Too many people fall short of realizing their career goals because they do not match their talents to their best career choices, or they sometimes fail to fully develop their aptitudes and apply them to appropriate career choices. I have also known many people who have underestimated their abilities and have, consequently, shortchanged themselves by not pursuing opportunities for which they were fully qualified.

Finally, look within yourself to creatively explore the many personal factors that bear on your career. Factors like dual career relationships, financial challenges, and geographic ties – to name a few – should be addressed realistically. We all have unique personal factors – some are helpful, and others are limiting – that must be considered in any career decision we make. The successful career planner realistically examines the limiting factors and leverages career advantages in a way to promote career development.

Step 2: Exploring Your Options

Only after you have looked within yourself and have gained insight about your career identity are you ready to begin exploring your options. I have always been surprised at how many people make a decision about their career without really understanding what they are getting into.

Often, in a desire to be rid of an uncomfortable career situation, people impulsively choose a career direction without gaining adequate information to assess whether it is appropriate for them. Or, they gravitate to a career choice without fully understanding its implications. One client, for example, pursued an extensive training program that qualified him for a management position at a resort. He surmised that a relaxed work atmosphere and being around people who were enjoying their leisure would help him find greater career satisfaction. What he did not consider, however, was that the job required him to work long hours, and to be frequently away from his family on weekends and holidays – requirements that were incompatible with his work values and that contributed to more career dissatisfaction than he previously had.

I expressed earlier my amazement over the detailed analysis and planning many people undertake when it comes to their vacations. Travel routes, comparative prices on accommodations, dining and entertainment options, and even the weather are fully scrutinized. Imagine if only we approached our careers in the same way.

A wealth of career information is available to help you make informed, sound, and strategic career decisions. The consequences of making ill-informed decisions include costly career setbacks. One of the most important career survival skills today is being able to find and use timely, high-quality career information. More than 10 years have elapsed since I wrote the first edition of *Decision Time: A Guide to Career Enhancement*, and I am astounded by how much more quality career-related information is readily available thanks to the Internet and advances in information technology.

The career information most beneficial to you will vary and depend upon the options you are considering. Information about wage and salary, training requirements for different occupations, and industry trends is always valuable when exploring career options. Labor market projections will help you understand the forecasted demand for workers in different occupations. Being able to find information on specific employers and jobs that offer opportunities consistent with your career needs, of course, can also enhance your decision making.

Some career decisions require even more specialized sources of career information, such as information on franchises, sources of capital for venture development, and information about career opportunities abroad. Whatever your career information needs, being able to secure accurate, current, and comprehensive information is vital. What you don't know can hurt you!

Step 3: Making Your Decision

After looking within yourself and gaining a thorough understanding of your options, you will be better equipped to make a career decision. As Figure 2 suggests, the decision-making model I use in my private work with clients calls for individuals to integrate self-information with information about specific options being considered. My emphasis at this point in the decision-making process is to keep clients focused on three critical factors:

- The risk they are realistically willing to assume in committing to a career decision.
- How likely they are to make changes in their career development, successfully.
- How fulfilling the potential change is likely to be.

Any career change you consider will involve at least some degree of risk. Later in the career change process, I have often found that those who were unsuccessful in moving forward with a career change were not honest with themselves in assessing the risk that they were really willing to assume.

While assessing your risk tolerance, it is essential that you realistically assess your chances for success in making potential career changes. That is, do you really possess the necessary aptitudes? How competitive are opportunities you may be seeking? What are your chances of prevailing over others who aspire to objectives similar to yours? Are the types of opportunities you seek plentiful, scarce, or even accessible to you? And, do you possess the resources necessary for success in the career paths you are contemplating, such as support of a significant other or financial resources that may be required to fund a business venture? Again, the answers to these and other questions material to your decision making are only within you.

Too often people wish to change careers not necessarily because they have researched and identified a more promising option, but because they consider their current career predicament to be unacceptable and sometimes downright aversive. The danger in "leaping before you look" from one unsatisfactory career path to another is high when you have not thoroughly assessed the potential for achieving greater fulfillment in your next career move. Before you commit to a career change make sure you know what it is you are getting yourself into!

Step 4: Career Planning

After you have made a career decision, it is time to plan how you are going to implement it. A good career plan is as vital to your career development as a blueprint is to building your home. It provides vision, structure, and direction; it can also serve as a motivational tool.

Thinking through the various details necessary to move ahead in your career development allows you to better use the resources available to you, strategically plan your actions, and take control of your career development. A good career plan outlines how you will move forward to accomplish your career goals. It also outlines back-up plans and serves as a tool to monitor your progress.

Step 5: Moving Ahead

Often the most difficult step in implementing a career decision is the first step – the one that moves you away from your current career path and into a new direction. Introspection and research, of course, lessen the risk of making an inappropriate career decision. There are no guarantees, however, that your next career move will enhance your present situation.

I sometimes think of those who persist in a career path in which they are very unhappy as similar to those who maintain a dysfunctional marriage or other undesirable relationship. Some people maintain these unions for fear of the unknown or concern that they will be even worse off if they risk change; similarly, those who hold onto unsatisfactory careers often share these same fears. At a personal level, the results of either a bad marriage or a poor person/job match are usually wrought with frustration, anger, and a compromised sense of fulfillment.

A good career plan can be invaluable in keeping you motivated and on track. Perhaps even more valuable, however, is a strong mentor – someone you respect and who has taken a genuine interest in your career goals and personal development. A discussion on how to develop a mentor/protégé relationship is presented later.

When you begin sensing a feeling of procrastination and complacency with moving ahead, do not allow yourself to be sidetracked from your career goals. Minor setbacks and unforeseen challenges will almost certainly arise.

Several years ago, I attended a business symposium in which a young, very successful CEO of a start-up communications technology company was a keynote speaker. After an impressive presentation, a member of the audience asked her to cite the most important lesson she learned as a businessperson. She instinctively replied, "Never lose sight of your vision and don't take ëno' for an answer." Taken at face value, a response of this type may sound trite. The conviction in her voice and the reflexive nature of her response, however, were testimony that her statement was truly a guiding force to her career success despite the obstacles she confronted along the way. This unwavering dedication and intensity is essential for you to maintain if you are to realize your most ambitious career goals.

Career Decision Making: A Never-Ending Process

Earlier, I said that career decision making tends to be a recurrent activity we engage throughout our youth and adult lives. For better or worse, you cannot simply make a career decision and then follow a straight path to your objective. During our careers, a myriad of events – often personal and sometimes even on a global level – invariably occurs and affects career plans. Our lives and the workplace are constantly in flux. The recycling arrows in Figure 2 suggest that the process of making and implementing a career decision is dynamic, and accounts for personal and workplace changes that alter the landscape of career choices for us to consider.

What may have been a good decision for you 25 years ago, 10 years ago, 5 years ago, or even 1 year ago may no longer be appropriate for you today. While relating how he felt his job as the chief information officer in a national transportation organization was no longer appropriate for him, one client mentioned how his preferences and priorities had changed over time while his job's characteristics and demands remained the same. Frequent travel, the need to work long hours with additional expectations of participating in industry and civic activities, and the pressure associated with keeping abreast with new technologies were no longer as compatible with his interests and lifestyle as they had been. This realization was an epiphany for the client: he had changed as a person yet his job had essentially not changed, and what had previously been a good match was no longer so.

Your career-related priorities are likely to change, just as your values, interests, skills, and personal circumstances may change and no longer remain ideally matched with career objectives you previously established and the path to attaining those objectives. Further, just as people change, so do their options. The organization in which you are employed is likely to change, the labor market changes, and so do technologies and methods of doing business. Some career options may no longer be viable as you look ahead; likewise, new career options are constantly arising.

Considering the intimate relationship between our career satisfaction and our overall quality of life, being able to make good career decisions and convert these decisions to advance your career development are two of the most important life survival skills you can develop. I hope the model presented in Decision Time will assist you not only with your pending career concerns and decisions, but also with future career decisions you will invariably face.

Please consider the following questions before proceeding to the next chapter.

- Are there economic, financial, technological, social or political factors in force that are affecting or likely will soon be affecting your career development? What implications do these forces hold? Below, identify the relevant forces and describe how they may affect your career.

- Consider the last two or three career decisions you made, and list them below. In retrospect, what elements of the decision-making model described in this chapter did you apply in these decisions? What elements did you omit? Could the quality of the decisions have been enhanced by more fully applying the model? If so, how? Assuming there are elements of the model that were not applied, what were they?

Chapter 3

❧

A Look Within

A Look Within

A Look Within

Career decisions are among the most important decisions we make. Our careers can affect virtually every area of our life, and the implications of poor decisions can be multifaceted and long lasting. Conversely, good quality career decisions can contribute to an enhanced lifestyle, positive self-concept, and fulfillment. This perspective is essential to *Decision Time: A Guide To Career Enhancement*.

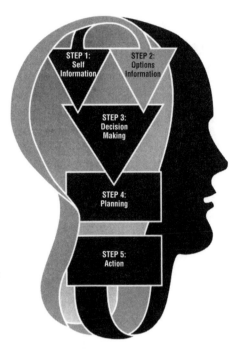

Complicating the career decision-making process are the many options from which to choose – the United States Department of Labor has identified more than 12,000 different occupations, and a myriad of nuances accompany each occupation. Our personal circumstances can further complicate our selection of career options and how we implement decisions. For example, in a situation involving a dual career couple, a job transfer affecting one partner can have significant implications on the career development of both partners.

We often have too little information on which to base our career decisions. Gathering the right kind of information starts with a close look within ourselves.

Approaching the career decision-making process by first identifying potential career options, and then sequentially evaluating and comparing them is tempting. Career counselors, however, believe that proceeding like this is premature. Rather, they recommend that you begin the process by looking within yourself. Focused and careful introspection can help you to gain insights that will enable you to better discern and assess important features of your career options that otherwise may be overlooked.

Unfortunately, too many people use an ongoing trial-and-error approach to their career development. They pursue one occupation or career path, move on to something else, and continue with a hit-or-miss approach to their career development through many frustrating years. If they are lucky, something along the way might work out for them. For those serious about their career development, however, this haphazard approach is unacceptable.

I am not suggesting that career experiences with less than positive outcomes have no value. Oscar Wilde put it well when he said, "Experience is the name we give to our mistakes." What I am suggesting is that a trial-and-error approach to your career development is likely to be more time consuming and wasteful than a systematic approach.

Many clients have suggested to me that they feel miscast in their careers almost as if they were playing an inappropriate role in a play: something is out of synch with the person-to-career match. Finding the right career fit begins with looking within.

Career Self-Analysis

There are four major areas in which I recommend you focus your self-analysis: your work values, your interests, your skills and aptitudes, and the personal circumstances that relate to your decision. We all have a career identity that is shaped by these four unique and very personal factors.

Our career identities change throughout our lives. At times, some aspects of your career identity can exert a stronger influence on your career development than others. I have often found that skills and interests strongly direct the career decision making of younger individuals, while typically the older and more evolved one's career, the more influential are work values and life circumstances. For instance, a young college graduate who is not in a relationship with a significant other, who possesses foreign language skills and an interest in living abroad, might choose to pursue career opportunities in foreign service or international business. On the other hand, a single parent of two young children may favor values such as a flexible work schedule and educational opportunity for his or her children when weighing career options.

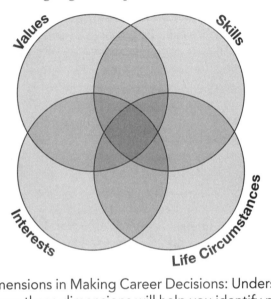

Figure 3: The four dimensions in Making Career Decisions: Understanding the shared aspects among these dimensions will help you identify potentially satisfying career options

Figure 3 includes a diagram providing a perspective that I recommend you consider as you consolidate your career identity. Each circle in intended to represent one of the four major areas that comprise your career identity. I encourage you to carefully define the composition of work values, interests, skills and aptitudes, and personal circumstances pertinent to your career decision making.

What is inside these areas varies from person to person. The challenge in looking within and discovering your true career identity is to find the common area where the four circles overlap. Also, remember that your career identity is always changing. The skills and career priorities you possessed a year ago, for example, are likely different than those you currently possess.

Good career decision making begins with putting forth an intense, honest effort to discover your career identity. Once you have been able to accomplish this, you are better equipped to research options that promise to be a strong match. The better the match, the better the chances for career fulfillment.

I have noticed that people often gain a sense of peace after they have discovered who they are in a career sense. This may contribute to research findings that college students who commit to a major area of study during their first or second years usually perform better scholastically than those who commit to a major later as juniors or seniors. Intuitively, we would expect people who have career goals and are attempting to progress toward them to perform better than their counterparts who lack this focus. Feeling out of control of your career development or not knowing where you are heading can be an overwhelming, unsettling experience.

This chapter will help you gain insight into your career identity. Each self-directed activity that follows will promote your exploration of important career considerations as you make decisions about your career.

Before you begin the following activities, use the space below to state as clearly as possible the issues that are motivating you to use *Decision Time*.

_____

_____

_____

_____

_____

_____

_____

_____

_____

Priorities: Focus on the Big Picture

The set of work values, or career priorities, we hold are shaped by many personal experiences throughout our lives. Our upbringing, life experiences, and education, for example, all contribute to our value systems. We each have a unique set of values. No value system is better or worse, right or wrong – just different.

Further, our values are always changing. Appreciating and articulating work values is not something most people formally attempt to do. Most have not really sat down and considered what is most important to them in their work and personal lives. They may have a generalized set of preferences that influence their decisions, but these preferences are often not defined well enough to aid in concrete career planning. The activity below will help you become aware of your most important work values.

While work values tend to vary widely among people, the world of work is, fortunately, diverse enough to accommodate the unique blend of values that most people hold. Sometimes people are bound to a career path that may have fit their values in the past, but is no longer appropriate for them because their career identities have changed and their present values are not necessarily in synch with their current career paths.

Realistically, finding an entirely complimentary match between your career options and your work values is rare. We learn at a very early stage in our lives and career development that, unfortunately, we cannot have everything we desire. But we can come close, perhaps, if we expend the effort to define our true priorities.

Every career choice that we encounter is likely to be fraught with trade-offs. A decision to pursue one career option may require you to forsake features of a different career option that you find appealing. By determining your most important work values, you can better evaluate the career options you are considering.

Values Survey

I developed the following survey to help you examine and prioritize what is really most important to you in your career. Please follow these instructions.

1. Refer to each value definition, and then rate the importance of each value to you in your career by circling from 0 to 5, the number which corresponds with the appropriate response ("prefer not to have" through "indispensable").

2. Place an asterisk (*) next to each work value that you rate either a 0, 1, or 2 if it is a significant feature of your current situation. Also, use the space on the far right side of the survey to make specific notes about work values that are particularly significant to your future career development or to indicate whether this value is being satisfied, as you desire, in your current job or life situation.

3. After you have finished the survey, refer to the questions that follow.

Figure 4: Career Values Survey

VALUE	Prefer Not To Have	Not Very Important	Would Be Nice	Very Important	Definitely A Priority	Can't Do Without	Notes
Achievement: Performing work that requires me to perform at my highest potential. Being results oriented.	0	1	2	3	4	5	
Adventure / Action: Work that sometimes offers excitement through risk, danger, or the unknown.	0	1	2	3	4	5	
Advancement Potential: A career path that offers opportunities for progressive growth through job titles, increased responsibilities, or greater earnings.	0	1	2	3	4	5	
Creativity: Using my imagination or creative talents to find new solutions to old problems.	0	1	2	3	4	5	
Location: Preferring an area because of accessibility to friends and relatives, climate, population, and size.	0	1	2	3	4	5	
High Income: Having enough money to significantly upgrade my lifestyle.	0	1	2	3	4	5	

VALUE	Prefer Not To Have	Not Very Important	Would Be Nice	Very Important	Definitely A Priority	Can't Do Without	Notes
High Intensity: Working under deadlines, demands, presssures, sometimes deriving glamour from work in exchange for making personal sacrifices.	0	1	2	3	4	5	
High Travel: Traveling frequently on job-related matters.	0	1	2	3	4	5	
Independence: Preferring unsupervised work, often making decisions on my own.	0	1	2	3	4	5	
Intellectual Stimulation: Using my mental abilities to solve problems and make decisions.	0	1	2	3	4	5	
Interaction With Others: Spending most of my day interacting with others.	0	1	2	3	4	5	
Leadership: A position in which I manage, supervise, or direct others.	0	1	2	3	4	5	
Leisure: Having the option of taking time away from work to pursue personal interests.	0	1	2	3	4	5	

VALUE	Prefer Not To Have	Not Very Important	Would Be Nice	Very Important	Definitely A Priority	Can't Do Without	Notes
Nontraditional Work: A job that, in some ways, is unique or different from most jobs performed in the labor market. Examples include clown, masseuse, escort.	0	1	2	3	4	5	
Personal Growth: Expanding self- and world awareness to enhance self-development.	0	1	2	3	4	5	
Professional Development: Developing new skills and increasing my competence through educational opportunities and work experience.	0	1	2	3	4	5	
Prestige: A position that offers status, respect, and influence.	0	1	2	3	4	5	
Recognition: Work activities that allow high visibility among coworkers and colleagues within my profession or community.	0	1	2	3	4	5	
Relationships Outside Work: Maintaining personal relationships in my free time.	0	1	2	3	4	5	

VALUE	Prefer Not To Have	Not Very Important	Would Be Nice	Very Important	Definitely A Priority	Can't Do Without	Notes
Responsibility: Being delegated duties that reflect others' trust in me, while being held accountable for accomplishments and mistakes.	0	1	2	3	4	5	
Security: Steadily employed in a stable work environment that is largely uninfluenced by economic, technological, or seasonal factors.	0	1	2	3	4	5	
Social Service: Work that allows me to either directly or indirectly improve the health, education, or welfare of others.	0	1	2	3	4	5	
Solitude: Working alone or with very little interaction with others.	0	1	2	3	4	5	
Unchanging Work Routine: Working in familiar situations and performing relatively routine, structured work.	0	1	2	3	4	5	
Variety: Exposure to new situations, people, and sometimes different work environments in which daily tasks are almost never the same.	0	1	2	3	4	5	

VALUE	Prefer Not To Have	Not Very Important	Would Be Nice	Very Important	Definitely A Priority	Can't Do Without	Notes
Working Conditions: Working in pleasant surroundings.	0	1	2	3	4	5	
Working as Part of a Team: Being dependent upon the input of and interaction with my coworkers.	0	1	2	3	4	5	

Values Survey Processing Questions

Please refer to your responses from the Values Survey as you complete the following steps and respond to the questions posed.

1. List below each of the work values that you rated as either 4 or 5. That is, those work values that you indicated were either definitely a priority or indispensable in your future career development.

_____

_____

_____

_____

_____

_____

_____

2. Next, refer to the values you listed above and rate each value in terms of its importance to you. That is, "1" for your most important work value, "2" for your second most important work value, etc. Your most important work value should appear at the top of your list, and your least important values from above should appear at the bottom of your list.

_____

_____

_____

_____

_____

_____

_____

3. Refer back to your responses from the Values Survey. Now, list each of the work values that you originally rated as either 0 or 1. That is, those values that you indicated you either prefer not to have or those that are not very important in your future career development.

_____

_____

_____

_____

_____

_____

_____

_____

4. Our work values often share common themes. For instance, common themes that
    we may be able to identify from someone who gave a very high rating to work values
    such as Achievement, High Income, Fast-Paced Lifestyle, and Prestige are the themes
    of motivation and high aspirations. Review the values that you listed in steps 2 and
    3 above. As you review your most important and least important work values, what
    common themes can you discern? Write the common themes you are able to glean
    from these values in the space below. Many readers find that completing this step
    with a career counselor, mentor, or an individual who knows you well is helpful.

Themes common among important work values:

_____

_____

_____

_____

Themes common among nonimportant work values:

_____

_____

_____

_____

_____

5. Consider your current career situation. To what degree can your most important work
    values be met in your current career path?

_____

_____

_____

_____

6. Use the space below to summarize what you have learned about your work values from this activity.

_____

_____

_____

_____

_____

_____

_____

7. What have you learned from this values exercise that you can use in making future career decisions? Summarize the most significant aspects of your work values on the worksheet on page 64 at the end of this chapter.

Discussion

After working through this exercise, many people find that they can more clearly identify what is important to them in their career development or, in some cases, what has been missing in their careers and contributing to lack of fulfillment. Others are able to confirm their thoughts about elements of their current situation that are lacking. Awareness is the first step to positive career change, and you are now well under way to knowing what you want in your future career development. Imagine developing your career with the opportunity to satisfy each of the values that you indicated you cannot do without. Now, let's move on and explore how your interests relate to various career options.

Interests: Will Your Choices Enhance Your Goals?

Many of us begin to feel pressure about making the "right" career decision at an early age. Decisions pertaining to education, occupation and job choice, and career development often seem ubiquitous. Many are haunted by the "what do you want to be when you grow up?" question throughout their career development.

I have always thought young people are particularly disadvantaged in dealing with the pressures associated with committing to a career decision. After all, few young people have had very much exposure to the world of work; most lack the information necessary to understand the options that may be compatible with their interests.

The importance of obtaining employment within a career direction that you find compatible with your interests – similar to our preceding discussion on work values – is central to your career fulfillment. Many times I have heard clients say, "I want a career, not a job." Implicit in this statement, I believe, is a plea to secure personally meaningful work that offers opportunities for further challenge and growth.

Drudgery – defined as being forced to perform hard, menial, or monotonous work – occurs when day in and day out, we engage in work that we find uninteresting, unchallenging, and unrewarding. Too many people seem resigned that "work" and "toil" are synonymous. They plod through their career development with a "work to live" mind set and, unfortunately, relinquish notions that work can enhance one's quality of life, assuming it is well matched for the individual.

As I mentioned earlier, the U.S. Department of Labor has classified more than 12,000 different occupations. This is obviously an overwhelming mass of career options for anyone to sort through and project whether their interests relate to different career options. While we all know that there are numerous options from which to choose, we sometimes feel that we have a limited or constricted awareness of what really is available to us. Fortunately, there is a popular classification system used by career counselors to help individuals better understand how their interests relate to career choices. This system is referred to as the "Holland Hexagon," developed by Dr. John Holland. In this section, we will examine your career interests and then, using the Holland system, relate your interests to various career options.

In both our work and leisure, some activities seem to interest us more naturally than others. Interests, like our work values, are derived from many sources. Needless to say, we usually find work that attracts and holds our interests more fulfilling than work that does not.

While you may be aware of your major interests, you probably have some undiscovered interests that, for many reasons, may be undeveloped. One way to broaden your awareness of these interests is to expose yourself to new experiences. For example, you can learn a great deal by initiating conversations about an average work day with people who are employed in jobs unfamiliar to you. Reading about various occupations, observing others as they perform their jobs, and volunteer work are other ways to become more aware of work tasks that may interest you. Although performing an activity is the best way to determine its appeal to you, you can also gauge your interests through activities of this sort.

The exercises that follow are designed to facilitate your self-exploration of your career interests.

Gaining Insight Into Your Career Interests

1. Please refer to Appendix A on page 119. Here you will find several pages listing titles of various occupations; brief descriptions of the occupations are on the opposite side. With a pair of scissors, cut out each of the cards along the dashed lines. When you are finished, each of the occupational titles will appear on rectangular pieces you have cut out.

2. Included among the cards of occupations that you cut out were four larger cards labeled "Very Interesting," "Interesting," "Somewhat Interesting," and "Uninteresting." Place each of these four category cards next to each other in four separate columns. Then, take the remaining rectangular cards that list the occupations you cut out and sort each of the cards into the respective columns according to how you feel about the occupation. You will need a large, flat surface for this activity.

3. Take the occupations that you classified under the "Uninteresting" category and group each of the occupations that you listed under this category into subgroups, which are based on the reasons these occupations are uninteresting to you. For example, your reasons could include: "Involves working with people," "Requires selling," "Involves Conflict," "Sounds too technical," "Low wages," "Don't like working with machines or equipment," or "Too much stress." There are no right or wrong ways to sort the cards; of course, your

reasons for your groupings is most important aspect. After you have grouped the occupations you have classified as uninteresting, list below the reasons for not choosing each subgroup of these occupations. Use one space for each subgroup that you form.

Uninteresting

Subgroup #1

Subgroup #2

Subgroup #3

Subgroup #4

Subgroup #5

Subgroup #6

4. Now take the occupations that you categorized under the "Somewhat Interesting" and "Interesting" columns. Just as you did above, combine these occupations into subgroups according to the reasons that you believe you find these occupations either interesting or somewhat interesting. After you have formed your subgroups, list below your reasons for finding each subgroup either interesting or somewhat interesting. Use one space for each subgroup that you formed.

Somewhat Interesting and Interesting

Subgroup #1

Subgroup #2

Subgroup #3

Subgroup #4

Subgroup #5

Subgroup #6

5. Now, take the remaining cards that you categorized under the "Very Interesting" column. Again sort these cards into subgroups related to why you believe these occupations are very interesting to you. When you are done, list below the reasons that you find each of the subgroups very interesting. Use one space for each subgroup that you formed.

Very Interesting

Subgroup #1

Subgroup #2

Subgroup #3

Subgroup #4

Subgroup #5

Subgroup #6

6. Compare your reasons for rejecting some occupations with your reasons for preferring other occupations. Try to label or describe in a few words and/or ideas that are suggested by your explanations for preferring or rejecting occupations. For example, you may prefer higher-level to lower-level occupations; the label or theme here is "My preference for prestige, higher salary, more education." Take your time as you try to identify themes that characterize why you chose or rejected the occupations from this activity.

Theme 1

Theme 2

Theme 3

Theme 4

Theme 5

Theme 6

Relating Interests to Career Options

As I mentioned above, a popular classification scheme for organizing occupations within the world of work was developed by Dr. John Holland. The Holland Hexagon is widely used to describe the relationship between interests in career choices. As its title implies, the Holland Hexagon uses a six-pointed scheme to organize the world of work. Each point on the hexagon corresponds to a cluster of occupations with a particular theme. A diagram of the Holland Hexagon with the corresponding titles of each family or cluster of occupations is in Figure 5.

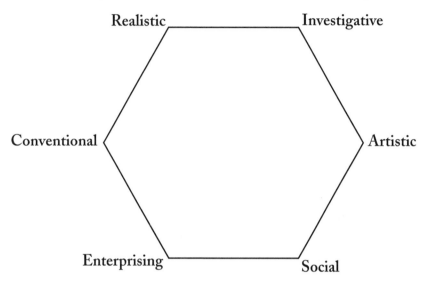

Figure 5. The Holland Hexagon

(NOTE: Reproduced by special permission of the Publisher, Psychological Assessment Resources, Inc., 16204 North Florida Avenue, Lutz, Florida 33549, from the *Self-Directed Search Professional Manual* by John L. Holland, Ph.D., copyright 1994. Further reproduction is prohibited without permission from PAR, Inc.)

Starting with the top left-hand point on the Holland Hexagon, the first family of occupations is referred to as **Realistic**. Generally, people who are attracted to Realistic occupations tend to be mechanically oriented. They quite often prefer activities involving using machines, tools, or technical instruments. They usually like to roll up their sleeves and get hands-on with their work. Many Realistic career options are in the construction, craft, repair, precision, and trades occupations. Also, many occupations involving the outdoors are within the Realistic family of occupations and include those in agriculture, animal sciences, and landscape architecture. People who are physically active and attracted to physically demanding activities are also often quite attracted to Realistic careers.

Moving clockwise on the Hexagon, the next family of occupations is referred to as **Investigative**. As the name implies, Investigative occupations quite often involve a high degree of analytical processes and research. Investigative occupations are often abundant the in sciences (environmental science, mathematics, physics, biology, genetics, etc.), information technology (programming, systems analyst, work engineering, Web design and maintenance, etc.), and healthcare. Among the healthcare occupations classified as Investigative are such diverse occupations as X-ray technologist, nurse, physicians' assistant, speech pathologist, optometrist, and pharmacist.

Continuing clockwise on the Hexagon, the next family of occupations is referred to as **Artistic**. Generally, people who are attracted to Artistic occupations prefer unstructured work. They prefer work that allows them to project their creativity into it. Such occupations can be found in advertising, fashion merchandising, and interior design. Also, many creative occupations exist in the visual arts, performing arts, graphic design, and writing.

The next family of occupations is referred to as **Social**. People attracted to Social career paths generally prefer work that involves promoting the health, education, or welfare of others. Examples of Social occupations include teaching, counseling, psychology, criminology, social work, religious occupations, and library science.

Moving on to the next family of careers is a cluster of occupations classified as **Enterprising**. Enterprising occupations usually involve some type of gain – such as power, influence, or financial – as a primary motivation for performing the work. Examples here include many occupations in politics, law, and business.

Finally, the sixth point on the Holland Hexagon references **Conventional** occupations. People attracted to Conventional occupations usually enjoy work that involves structure, precision, and attention to detail. Administrative occupations, accounting, computer programming, drafting, and many occupations related to financial services are classified as conventional.

As you read the descriptions of the six major families of careers classified in the Holland Hexagon, you most likely identified features of various occupational clusters that sounded relevant to your career interests. Some areas, however, were probably more descriptive of you than others. The notion underlying the Holland system is that we all have a combination of features from the six families of occupations within our vocational profile; however, some features are more dominant or expressed than others. And, just as people have a unique vocational profile, so do occupations in the world of work. The objective is to understand how our vocational profile, as identified by our Holland Type, relates to the six different areas, and then to relate our Holland type to career choices. The *Self-Directed Search,* first published by Dr. John Holland in 1972 and most recently revised in 1994, is an assessment instrument that can help you more clearly identify your Holland Type. A qualified career counselor can administer and interpret it for you.

If you want to explore this further, see Holland, John L., "*Self-Directed Search,* 1994 Revision." This is a self-marking test which you can use to discover your "Holland Code" and what occupations you might start your research with. You can order an SDS specimen set for $10 plus shipping and handling from the publisher, Psychological Assessment Resources, Inc., 16204 North Florida Avenue, Lutz, Florida 33549 (or call toll free 1-800-331-TEST). This set includes the SDS Assessment Booklet, Occupations Finder, You and Your Career Booklet, Leisure Activities Finder, and Educational Opportunities Finder. You may also take the SDS online for $9.95 and receive a report. The Web site address is www.self-directed-seacrch.com.

Interest Survey Processing Questions

1. As you consider the Holland classification system, which of the six families of occupations do you believe are most in line with your interests? In the space below, list what you believe to be the top three Holland families as they relate to your interests and your reasons for your selections.

Highest Holland area

Second highest Holland area

Third highest Holland area

2. Refer to your "Very Interesting" responses on pages 35-36. As you review your rationale for grouping occupations into the Very Interesting category, how would you classify each of the occupations according to the six Holland themes? Which three Holland themes best describe each occupation?

3. Appendix B lists occupations that are classified by Holland Type. The occupations are listed according to the first letter of the respective Holland Hexagon family of careers. The positioning of the three-letter coding is significant. The fist letter indicates the dominant theme within the occupational title. The second letter indicates the next most dominant theme, followed by the third letter, which indicates the third most dominant theme within the respective occupational title. Review the various occupations that fall within your three-letter code that you indicated is most characteristic of your interests. Also, examine permutations of the three top Holland themes that you believe to be most expressed in your Holland code. List below all the occupations that you find interesting under those for your codes.

4.   As in the earlier exercise in which you sorted occupations into groups and subgroups according to related characteristics, organize the occupations you listed in question 3 above into categories based upon your belief of why you find these occupations interesting. Also, refer to the occupations you rated as Very Interesting on pages 35-36 and organize these occupations in the same way. Write your reasons for your choices in the space below.

5.   Summarize the most significant aspects of your interests on the worksheet on page 64 at the end of this chapter.

Discussion

I hope this activity helped you to consolidate your career identity. Our work has thus far concentrated on helping you to more clearly define your work values and priorities, as well as identify occupations compatible with your interests. I surmise that you have become aware of at least a few new occupations that have raised your curiosity; a few career options you have already considered were likely among those that appeared as you completed the Interest Activity. Your career identity is probably starting to become more clear to you. Let's move ahead to the next section and examine your skills and aptitudes, so we can further clarify your career identify.

Do You Have What it Takes? Reviewing Your Skills

You have probably read or heard accounts by workplace columnists, business leaders, and career development professionals predicting how the workplace will look in the decade ahead. More than 10 years have passed since I wrote the first edition of *Decision Time: A Guide To Career*

Enhancement, and I now have the benefit of being able to assess the experts' accuracy. For the most part, they were on target! Futurists were accurate in their projections, for example, of large job growth in the healthcare, information technology, and service industries. Other accurate projections pertain to the globalization of our workplace, corresponding with a constriction in the U.S. manufacturing sector. From a skills perspective, experts' forecasts invariably project a much more specialized future workforce that will develop increasingly specific skill sets. The trend toward lifelong learning is well established, and technological advances, including distance learning opportunities, have helped to limit accessibility barriers that previously prevented many from acquiring new skills. You can be certain, in the decade ahead, that even more specialized and sophisticated skills will be in demand, and savvy career planners will be mindful of this – lest they choose to compromise their future opportunities and career satisfaction. Generally, writing, oral communication, analytical skills, problem-solving skills, and critical thinking skills are projected to be among those in greatest demand in tomorrow's workplace.

I have found that people often discount or take for granted the skills they have developed through their education, training, employment, and other life experiences. Further, we often undervalue the skills we possess. Even if you no longer wish to apply the various skills you have already developed as you look ahead in your career development, identifying and assessing the skills you have cultivated is important to determine whether they can be transferred or built upon so as to allow you to pursue alternate career opportunities.

There are many ways to identify your skills and aptitudes. You can think of a skill as an ability you have already developed to some level of expertise, while an aptitude is a capacity or potential you may have yet to develop and convert. Standardized tests are used commonly by career counselors to identify areas of strengths and weaknesses within an individual. These tests help determine your levels of competence and expertise in diverse areas such as mechanical reasoning, visual analysis, inductive and deductive reasoning, verbal abilities, quantitative skills, manual speed and dexterity, and attention to detail. To be sure, there are thousands of tests available to assess numerous skills and aptitudes. In depth assessment of your skills and aptitudes is best advised when considering a major career change in which retraining is a likelihood.

Decision Time includes a measure of abilities to help you become more aware of the skills you have developed through your most significant career and personal accomplishments. One effective way to better understand your set of skills is to examine one of your major accomplishments, and then breakdown each of the individual skills that were required. I recall one client, a computer programmer, whom I assisted in my counseling practice. She described a sophisticated computer system she developed and implemented to track the sales histories of key client accounts. As we discussed the scope of this project, she realized many diverse skills were required for her success. Besides the technical skills associated with developing the software, she realized that she also employed advanced skills related to documentation, designing, imagining, persuading, project management, and training.

Figure 6 provides examples of my analyses of transferable skills developed by several clients I have counseled. Often, people have difficulty discerning their most valuable skills and identifying how they may be of value in environments other than those in which they have previously worked.

Figure 6 Examples of Significant Transferable Skills

Client 1: A 53-year-old high school graduate who pursued college studies but did not satisfy requirements necessary to earn a degree. The work history she presented pertained to employment in sales and marketing positions, primarily in the architecture, construction, and engineering industries.

Primary skills: Marketing professional services; operating Windows software; researching marketing trends and business development opportunities; building client relationships; technical knowledge specific to architecture, engineering, and construction; writing proposals; technical writing; reviewing proposals for grammar and sentence structure; making sales and marketing presentations; training technical staff; prospecting clients; administering an annual budget between $2 million and $5 million; and supervising a market coordinator and an intern.

Client 2: A 42-year-old individual who earned an MBA degree at an Ivy League school and presented a record of progressive advancement in executive level positions at two Fortune 500 organizations.

Primary skills: Public speaking; training and facilitation; technical writing; financial analysis; strategic planning; diagnosing business problems; factory management; inventory control; leadership; environmental and quality engineering; operations management; quality management; procurement (manufacturing); plant management; and negotiating with vendors.

Client 3: A 33-year-old high school graduate with a work history related to truck driving and raising, showing, and maintaining horses.

Primary skills: Operating semitrailer trucks; horse maintenance including training and farrier skills; valuing, buying, selling, and shoeing horses; purchasing, using, and maintaining horse equipment such as harnesses, farm implements, manure spreaders, cultivators, and mowing machines; general farming including raising up to 70 heads of cattle; supervising up to 12 hitch hands; planning horse operations such as breeding, security, and hitch programs; operating special equipment on semitrailers including large hoses to unload freight such as oxygen, helium, and various chemicals; German language skills; and bartending.

Client 4: A 29-year-old individual who completed an associate of arts degree related to air-conditioning and heating technology, and later pursued employment as a code enforcement officer with a municipality.

Primary skills: Responding to complaints from the public about housing and sanitation code violations; knowledge of construction problems concerning structural, electrical, plumbing, and air conditioning/heating; blueprint reading and architectural drawing; documenting compliance problems; enforcing compliance; educating code violators; preparing inspection reports; participating in adjudication of code violators, including presenting cases in front of a special master; and customer service.

Client 5: A 46-year-old high school graduate who had approximately 20 years of experience working in law firms, most recently as an accounts receivable clerk.

Primary skills: Data entry of disbursements, cash receipts, wire transfers, and checks; processing checks for deposit; reconciling account balances; typing 65–70 words per minute; general office administration; and using a proprietary billing application at her former place of employment.

Ironically, we sometimes develop a great deal of expertise in an area in which we have no interest whatsoever in continuing our career development. I have counseled many individuals with outstanding administrative and clerical skills, for instance, who have no interest at all in continuing their careers in this direction, despite the expertise they have acquired. I often find that many people have had limited career options available to them. Consequently, they develop a career path and accompanying skills in an area that became readily available to them, rather than an area that they actively sought. Even if this situation is familiar to you and you do not wish to use the primary skills you have already developed, there is value in examining the skills you already possess, as well as those that you would like to further develop.

Identifying the skills that you already possess, as well as those you would like to further develop, can be invaluable in your career planning and decision making. You can polish and refine almost any type of skill by investing in further education and training, observing those who are already expert in the skill that you wish to further develop, looking for opportunities to practice and hone your skills, and being coached by others.

I have found that attitudes often get in the way of our ability to refine old skills and develop new ones. We sometimes set our own limits in our self-development because a) we do not value our work, b) a low self-esteem robs our initiative to enhance our skill set, or c) the prospect of change can be overwhelming and seem like too much work (too often, complaining and coasting are easier than learning new skills – just like it is sometimes easier to stay in established relationships than to develop new ones). If you are experiencing self-esteem problems, you will probably discount your skills and accomplishments. It is also possible that your skills are not valued in your current job. If this is the case, your challenge might be to promote the value and application of your skill set at your current place of employment or elsewhere.

The Skills Activity that follows is designed to stimulate your thinking about the skills you already possess as well as those you wish to develop further. You will also find the Skills Activity valuable in isolating and describing your skills as you prepare resumes in the future. Extensive work experience can be condensed and summarized into groups of skills headings under a "Qualifications" or "Summary of Significant Skill Areas" section of a resume. The skills assessment activity, which follows, can also help you to organize your response to interview questions by focusing on past work accomplishments.

Skills Activity

The following space is for you to list five of the most significant accomplishments you have achieved during the past 5 years. You can list both career as well as personal accomplishments as you choose. The order in which you list your accomplishments should reflect relative importance to you. Your most significant accomplishment will be listed first, your second most significant accomplishment will be listed second, etc. As you list your accomplishments, please be as specific as possible. For example, write, "Initiated a customer service program that reduced complaints by 26% and saved my company $150,000, annually" rather than "Customer service." After you identify your accomplishment, write down all of the things you did to realize it. This will help you to be more accurate and comprehensive as you work through the activity. I recommend that you first put Decision Time aside for a few minutes and reflect back on your life accomplishments before you proceed.

While reflecting on past accomplishments, do not restrict yourself to thinking about accomplishments from school or work. For example, one client cited his involvement in his church's capital development campaign, and he identified several skills that made the effort successful. Avocational activities, family activities, and other personal endeavors are fair game to consider for this exercise.

Accomplishment #1

Accomplishment #2

Accomplishment #3

Accomplishment #4

Accomplishment #5

To a degree, the accomplishments you chose likely reflect your work values. Would your boss, best friend, parent, or significant other be likely to list the same accomplishments as you? What is it about these particular accomplishments that make them important to you? Write your response below.

_____

_____

_____

_____

_____

You can categorize your skills into seven major areas:
- Physical and mechanical skills
- Thinking and reasoning skills
- Creative and judgment skills
- Interpersonal skills
- Self-management skills
- Detail skills
- Quantitative skills

In the checklist that follows, mark the skills that you used to attain each of the accomplishments you listed. Then, review the checklist again – this time checking the skills you would like to develop in your future work. Also, for each of the skills you checked, indicate your level of proficiency in using that skill as high, medium, or low.

Figure 7: Skills Checklist

SKILL	ACCOMPLISHMENTS					WISH TO DEVELOP	LEVEL OF PROFICIENCY		
	#1	#2	#3	#4	#5		HIGH	MEDIUM	LOW
Physical and Mechanical Skills									
1. Adjusting – Fine-tuning a mechanical device or object to improve performance.									
2. Assembling – Constructing, taking apart objects.									
3. Endurance – Withstanding adversity or stress.									
4. Finger Dexterity – using your fingers with precision.									
5. Manual Dexterity – Using your hands with presicion.									
6. Operating – Physically controlling or guiding machines, tools, or equipment.									
7. Physical Coordination – Performing skilled and coordinated movements and motor activities to a single end.									
8. Rapid Reaction – Responding quickly.									
9. Strength – Performing heavy physical labor.									
Thinking and Reasoning									
10. Analyzing – Breaking down a problem into its different factors and parts, and examining each part independently.									

SKILL	ACCOMPLISHMENTS					WISH TO DEVELOP	LEVEL OF PROFICIENCY		
	#1	#2	#3	#4	#5		HIGH	MEDIUM	LOW
Thinking and Reasoning cont.									
11. Designing – Conceiving and planning an idea.									
12. Developing – Building on an idea to improve or refine it.									
13. Evaluating – Assessing the outcome of a product or program.									
14. Imagining – Creating a future vision.									
15. Planning – Arranging events according to an overall design or objective.									
16. Research – Gathering relevant information systematically and efficiently.									
17. Structuring – Organizing information into patterns, categories, or systems.									
18. Synthesizing – Restructuring existing knowledge, ideas, and concepts into new ones. Creating new information and concepts.									
Creative and Judgment Skills									
19. Aesthetic Judgment – Demonstrating appreciation for beauty.									
20. Color Discriminaton – Differentiating among colors.									

SKILL	ACCOMPLISHMENTS					WISH TO DEVELOP	LEVEL OF PROFICIENCY		
	#1	#2	#3	#4	#5		HIGH	MEDIUM	LOW
Creative and Judgment Skills cont.									
21. Depth Perception – Judging distances of objects and their spatial relationships.									
22. Shape Descrimination – Differentiating forms, sizes, and textures.									
23. Sound Discrimination – Differentiating among sounds.									
Interpersonal Skills									
24. Conflict Resolution – Taking action to relieve tension between people.									
25. Cooperating – Coordinating details with others to achieve a common goal.									
26. Crisis Management – Performing under extreme stress or unfavorable conditions.									
27. Counseling – Facilitating others' self-exploration and providing guidance in decision making.									
28. Editing – Improving the quality of a written or oral communication.									
29. Helping – Treating someone to relieve physical or emotional pain. Showing under-standing, regard, and acceptance.									

SKILL	ACCOMPLISHMENTS					WISH TO DEVELOP	LEVEL OF PROFICIENCY		
	#1	#2	#3	#4	#5		HIGH	MEDIUM	LOW
Interpersonal Skills cont.									
30. Initiating – Starting and cultivating new relationships.									
31. Negotiating – Bargaining to reach agreement.									
32. Performing – Carry on an action before a group.									
33. Persuading – Influencing attitudes or behaviors.									
34. Pleasing – Satisfying others' needs and desires.									
35. Reading – Comprehending written information.									
36. Supervising – Directing others to take responsibilty for their performance.									
37. Teaching / Training – Facilitating learning.									
38. Writing – Composing ideas that are expressed through print or sound media.									
Self-Management Skills									
39. Accepting Instructon and Evaluation – Modifying your ideas or behavior on the basis of others' advice or suggestions.									
40. Conforming – Following and supporting rules, policies, and guidelines.									

SKILL	ACCOMPLISHMENTS					WISH TO DEVELOP	LEVEL OF PROFICIENCY		
	#1	#2	#3	#4	#5		HIGH	MEDIUM	LOW
Self-Management Skills cont.									
41. Decision Making – Selecting an action plan and taking responsibility.									
42. Dependability – Demonstrating reliability and trustworthiness.									
43. Diligence – Persisting energetically toward a goal.									
44. Drive – Having strong motivation.									
45. Delaying Gratification – Persisting in a task that grants little initial reward.									
46. Integrity – Making decisions on moral or ethical basis.									
47. Performing Under Pressure – Responding appropriately in situations involving stress.									
48. Risk Taking – Assuming tasks that could result in significant gain or loss.									
49. Self-Control – Keeping your composure in stressful or adverse situations.									
50. Time Management – Scheduling and performing your activities efficiently.									
51. Tolerating Repetition – Persistent in a monotonous task.									

SKILL	ACCOMPLISHMENTS					WISH TO DEVELOP	LEVEL OF PROFICIENCY		
	#1	#2	#3	#4	#5		HIGH	MEDIUM	LOW
Self-Management Skills cont.									
52. Versatility – Demonstrating flexibility in using many skills.									
53. Working Under Adversity – Working under unpleasant physical, social, or psychological conditions.									
Detail Skills									
54. Attention to Detail – Responding to many intricacies involved in completing a task.									
55. Categorizing – Organizing information, data, or objects.									
56. Caution – Evaluating risks before making a committment.									
57. Following Directions – Carrying out others' instructions.									
58. Precision – Attending to details accurately.									
59. Projecting – Anticipating outcomes and potential scenarios.									
60. Record Keeping – Documenting the flow of information, finances procedures, objects, or ideas.									
61. Thoroughness – Monitoring a project's progress from beginning to end.									

SKILL	ACCOMPLISHMENTS					WISH TO DEVELOP	LEVEL OF PROFICIENCY		
	#1	#2	#3	#4	#5		HIGH	MEDIUM	LOW
Detail Skills cont.									
62. Verifying – Reviewing for accuracy.									
Quantitative Skills									
63. Accounting – Keeping track of financial transactions.									
64. Budgeting – Planning and allocating finances.									
65. Calculating – Making mathematical computations.									
66. Estimating / Cost Analsis – Undergoing analysis to precisely appraise values.									
67. Measuring – Using an instrument or procedure to ascertain dimensions, quantity, or capacity.									
68. Data and Statistical Analysis – Using mathematical or statistical procedures to analyze data and to solve problems.									

SKILL AREAS	RATING AMONG PEERS								
	TOP 1% (truly exceptional)	TOP 10% (superior)	TOP 20% (out-standing)	TOP 33% (above average)	LOWER 50% (average)	LOWER 40% (slightly below average)	LOWER 33% (poor)	LOWER 10% (very poor)	
Physical and Mechanical Abilities									
Thinking and Reasoning Skills									
Creative Judgment Skills									
Interpersonal Skills									
Self-Management Skills									
Detail Skills									
Quantitative Skills									
Other									

Skills Survey Processing Questions

The preceding worksheet will help you to compare your perception of how your skills relate to those of your peers. Indicate your opinions of how your skills compare with those who are the same age, have the same educational background, and the same levels of experience as you. Then, respond to the following questions:

1. Review the skills that you indicated were critical to attaining your major life accomplishments that you listed on page 44. What common features do the skills you checked share? How have you developed the most prominent skills that comprise your skill set? Of all the skills you identified, which do you feel are your strongest? List those skills below.

2. The way we rate ourselves as compared to others of the same age, education, and level of experience can sometimes provide insight into our self-concepts. For instance, people who consistently rate themselves at a lower level than their peers quite often show evidence of a low self-esteem and a tendency to devalue themselves. On the other hand, those who rate themselves consistently very high sometimes show evidence of an inflated self-esteem or over-valued self-worth. As you review how you rated your skills as compared to your peers, how consistent are your self-ratings with the comments and reactions from others? You might find it helpful to have someone who knows you well comment on your self-ratings, and then request feedback on how that person would rate you. List any discrepancies between your own ratings and the perceptions of others in the space below.

3.   Using the skills you listed in question 1 (those skills you identified as your strongest), compare your level of expertise in each skill to the expertise of your peers (again, those who are comparable in terms of experience and education) according to the scale below. List the skills next to the appropriate scale rating.

Top 1% (truly exceptional)

Top 10% (superior)

Top 20% (outstanding)

Top 33% (above average)

Top 50% (average)

Lower 40% (slightly below average)

Lower 33% (poor)

Lower 10% (very poor)

4.   In the space below, list each skill that you checked in the "Wish to Develop" column. After you have completed your list, place a star (*) next to those skills that are priorities for you to develop in the next 6 to 12 months.

_____

_____

_____

_____

_____

_____

_____

5. Use the space below to write what you have learned about your skills through this exercise.

_____

_____

_____

_____

6. On the worksheet on pages xxx through xxx at the end of this chapter, summarize the most significant aspects of your skills.

Discussion

How difficult was it for you to identify your noteworthy accomplishments? Many clients find it useful to evaluate their skill sets from a competitive perspective; that is, weighing the skills you possess against those who are already embarked in the career path that you are considering. I recommend that you keep a list of accomplishments that are important to you – both work-related and otherwise – and conduct this type of activity every few years.

Creating Opportunities: The Personal Side

Often, nothing influences our career development more than our personal circumstances, the hand that fate has dealt us, or we sometimes choose it ourselves. This may include things such as good or poor health, acquiring disabling problems, growing up in an advantaged or disadvantaged family, having attachments and bonds to people and settings in a particular geographic area, having children in school and being apprehensive about moving them, leaving aging parents or grandparents, and enjoying the comfortable benefits package at your current place of employment, while second guessing yourself about giving up those benefits or a career change.

Life circumstances can be like the proverbial double-edged sword: some can be very constraining, while others, if used properly, can open wide doors to our futures. The key is to take candid stock of the downside of your life circumstances while planning a strategy to creatively harness the life circumstances that could aid your career development.

The term *golden handcuffs* is used sometimes to describe personal circumstances that impact our career development. The term is a paradox. On one hand, these life circumstances are helpful; on the other hand, they are limiting. Consider life circumstances such as being vested in your company's retirement program, having children that are in school or college, and having worked your way up the career ladder at your present organization to the point where you enjoy benefits such as a generous vacation and a comfortable compensation package. Or in the case of a college student, weighing the merits of further education against the prospect of the long-term repayment of student loans. These life circumstances are golden, or desirable, in the sense that they provide a degree of creature comfort. At the same time, however, the circumstances are a handcuff, or disincentive to career change, in that they can make it difficult to leave a less than ideal person/job match. Sometimes staying in a job for too long can have negative effects on one's self-esteem and work productivity. Take heed if you hear yourself saying, "I can't afford to leave my job."

In our overall analysis of life circumstances, we typically find that we have a combination of limiting or challenging life circumstances, along with golden handcuffs that sometimes anchor us in a career path in which we are not fulfilled. We typically acquire more golden handcuffs as our careers mature. I have found that quite often people either become intimidated by or overestimate the degree of limitation that various life circumstances pose. They also tend to overlook or underestimate the power and resources available to them through their life circumstances.

The most common limiting factor to making a career change is often related to financial security. When people tolerate an undesirable work situation in exchange for an attractive salary and other financial trappings, they are both positioning and leaving themselves vulnerable to the ill effects of prostitution.

Of course, we would all be incredibly naive to overlook the influence of financial security in a career decision. I have found, however, that too often the fear of jeopardizing one's financial security casts an overly limiting influence that sometimes causes people to prematurely dismiss any further thoughts of a career change. Financial concerns are invariably addressed during career counseling; my usual practice is to recommend that clients do two things. First, I recommend that they draft a budget and cash flow analysis of their financial needs. Second, I recommend that they develop a concrete plan with a realistic time frame to allow them to make the lifestyle transition that may be necessary during their career change. Resources are sometimes available that we may not have considered or may have underestimated. Part-time work, securing monies from community sources, borrowing from a bank or relative – they are but few of the many resources that may be available to help sustain you during a period of career transition when you anticipate a diminution in your income.

My advice is to always be realistic in assessing your financial needs while, at the same time, not allowing yourself to be held captive to financial concerns that impact your career decision making. I sometimes refer to the "Tarzan Principle" of career development: Never let go of a good grip on a vine (or a secure career position) until you have a firm grip on another vine (or a promising career alternative).

We all have a different set of life circumstances that influences our career development. On a positive side, factors such as a very supportive spouse, access to influential people through family or business contacts, good control over your financial situation, and being physically fit can be advantages to your career development. As the saying goes, "Beauty is in the eyes of the beholder." This is the outlook I recommend you take when assessing your life circumstances.

Many of the circumstances that we believe have either a positive or negative influences on our career development are largely psychologically based. For instance, no matter how much net worth some people accumulate, they maintain a cautious lifestyle and carefully watch every dime and nickel they spend. Others, sometimes overly optimistically, live well beyond their means and have no concerns whatsoever about their finances. Is one approach right or wrong? My purpose is not to answer this question but to provoke your own thinking about your disposition on the effects of your financial resources and other personal circumstances on your career development.

Only you can define what is an asset and what is a true limitation or challenge to your career options. No one else can make this judgment. The exercises that follow will help you to examine the effect various life circumstances have had on you historically. You will also examine factors that could be either limiting or helpful as you look ahead to your career development.

Assessing Life Circumstances

1a. We can learn a great deal about ourselves by examining various patterns that have characterized our career development. The next exercise will allow you to examine your "career lifeline." First, in the spaces that follow, list at least 10 major career milestones that you can identify in reflecting back on your career development. A career milestone could be an event such as moving away to attend school, getting discharged from the armed services, starting your own business, getting fired from a job, dropping out of school, getting your first job, or getting promoted. The milestones you list will most likely be both positive and negative in terms of their effect on your personal and career development. As you reflect on your career to date, what stands out? Try to recall as many significant events as possible, beginning with the end of your high school years. Be particularly attentive to significant career events that occurred within the past 10 years.

Milestone 1

_____

Milestone 2

_____

Milestone 3

_____

Milestone 4

_____

Milestone 5

_____

Milestone 6

_____

Milestone 7

_____

Milestone 8

_____

Milestone 9

_____

Milestone 10

_____

1b. Refer to the "Career Lifeline" diagram in Figure 9. You will use this diagram to chart the ups and downs of your career development according to the career milestones you listed in part 1a. To do this, think of the horizontal line going across the page as a baseline or neutral point in terms of how you view the outcome of a career milestone. The Career Lifeline has two dimensions. First, consider the area above the horizontal line as the positive direction. The higher above the baseline that you graph a career milestone, the more positive its rating; that is, the more positive the impact the career milestone had on your career development. On the other hand, the space below the baseline or horizontal line refers to negative outcomes of your career development. In the same way, the lower that you graph a career milestone below the baseline, the more negative the impact the career milestone had on your career development.

The second dimension on the career lifeline is related to time. Points on the left side of the lifeline should present past events in your life; as you move across the baseline from left to right you are moving from past events to those in the present. A sample career lifeline is provided for your reference in Figure 8. As you can see from this sample lifeline, the individual who completed it identified several ups and downs in their career development. Use a pencil to construct your career lifeline on the diagram that appears in Figure 9. Plot the career milestones you listed in Part 1a onto the lifeline diagram provided. Remember – the higher above the baseline that you plot a career milestone, the more positive was its impact on your career development; the lower below the baseline, the more negative the impact on your career development. After you have plotted your career milestones, connect the points. You should end your diagram with your current life situation.

Life Circumstances Processing Questions

1. We can sometimes detect themes as we examine patterns within our career lifeline. For instance, some people might note a somewhat consistent interval that is interspersed between periods of high and low points. Other people may note some commonalities among the high points, and some commonalities among the low points in their career lifelines. For example, the high points are getting higher over time; relationships that have a major influence on the outcome of a career milestone; low points are usually characterized by not being in control of your career direction. In examining your own career lifeline, what common themes can you detect? How would you rate yourself in terms of risk-taking propensity? When you did take a degree of risk in your career development, and what was the outcome? How influential have other people been in the career decisions you have made? Use the following space to write your observations from your analysis of your career lifeline.

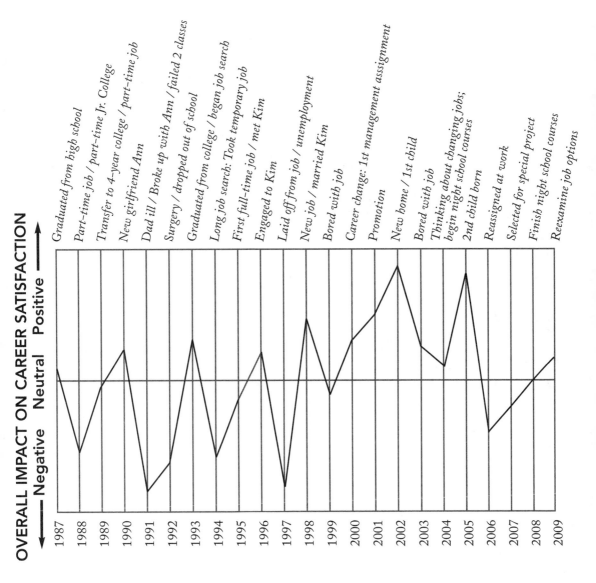

Figure 8. Sample career lifeline

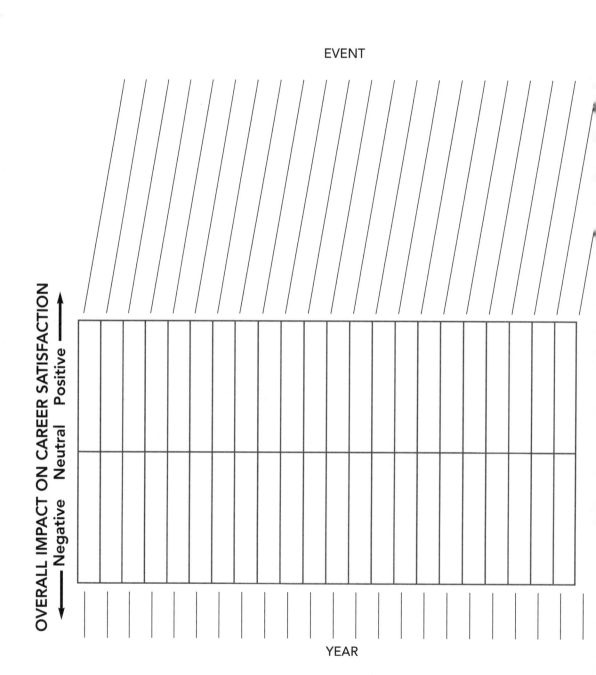

Figure 9. Your career lifeline

2. On the next page you will find a list of personal factors that can sometimes have significant implications on your career development. In examining this list you may identify some personal factors that are potentially very helpful to your future career development, while others may be somewhat limiting. For example, a good friend or partner can be an invaluable asset to your career development by supporting your goals, helping with finances, and assuming some of your responsibilities, thereby allowing you more time to pursue your career objectives. On the other hand, a personal factor such as a disability that restricts your mobility and functional capacities could be limiting. Use the space provided to respond to the personal factors that are listed in terms of the helpful or potentially limiting effect they may have on your career development. Be sure to list other factors not noted that might also impact on your career decision; be as thorough as possible and write your rationale for classifying a personal factor in either the helpful or limiting column in the space that is provided. After you have finished, continue with the questions that follow:

PERSONAL FACTOR	EFFECT ON CAREER PLANNING	
	HELPFUL	LIMITING
Financial Status		
Relationships		
Health		
Labor Market Outlook		
Family Expectations		
Societal Stereotyping		
Available Opportunities		
Personal Commitment to Change		
Education / Training		
"Golden Handcuffs"		
Other		
Other		
Other		

3. How can you harness the potentially positive affect of the personal factors you identified as being helpful to your career development? For instance, if you are fortunate to have a supportive partner and an above average financial situation, you may be able to open new career opportunities by cutting back on your current work responsibilities and pursuing activities to enhance your skill set. Identify as many specific actions as possible that you can take to help you leverage the potentially helpful affect of these factors. Use the space below to summarize your ideas.

4. As you examine the personal factors that you identified as being potentially limiting, realistically appraise each limiting factor and assess the degree to which these factors could impede your career development. Use the following space to record your thoughts.

5. What actions, if any, can you take to dispel or neutralize the impact of the potentially limiting personal factors that you have identified? Actions you may consider include attending personal development workshops, participating in counseling, pursuing specialized training, and repositioning your finances. Record your thoughts below.

6. Taken together, what overall affect do the personal factors (both helpful and limiting) in your life have on your future career development? Provide your analysis in the space below.

7. Summarize the most significant aspects of your personal circumstances on the worksheet on page 64.

Discussion

We have completed our career-related self-analysis by focusing on patterns that have influenced our career development to date, and personal factors that are important to consider as we begin to identify viable career options – the next task we will undertake. Your career identity – composed of your work values, interests, skills, and life circumstances – should be much clearer after having completed the activities contained in this chapter. Again, many people find it helpful to further discuss what you have learned with a career counselor, mentor, or someone who knows you well. Having a solid grounding on who you are, from a career sense, is essential to making good quality career decisions and managing your subsequent career development.

Summary of Career Self-Analysis Activities

The exercises contained in this chapter have hopefully helped you to look within yourself as you consider your career development. Use the worksheet that follows to summarize what you have learned from your self-analysis.

The values most important to me are

My major interests involve

My strengths and skills include

The skills I wish to further develop are

The actions I can take to better use personal circumstances are

My career aspirations include

Chapter 4

◈

Understanding Your Options

Understanding Your Options

A few years ago, a large professional association composed of practicing lawyers contacted me and requested that I conduct a career planning seminar titled "Lawyers in Transition." The focus of this seminar, I was informed, would be to provide professional guidance to lawyers who were considering leaving the profession. Two questions struck me when I received the request. First, why would a professional association sponsor a program to help its members leave the profession? Second, because attending this public seminar could have devastating effects on attendees' future careers in law if they decide not to change careers and remain within the legal profession, who would come?

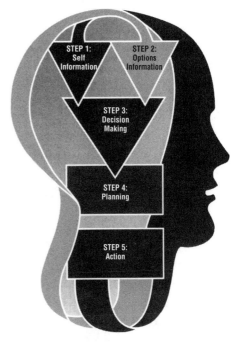

You can imagine my surprise the morning of the seminar when more than 50 attorneys – each seriously considering leaving the profession in which they heavily invested in terms of education, time, and finances – registered for the program. To me, these individuals represented a fragment of attorneys who were also malcontent in their career development. Those in attendance were probably experiencing a great deal of "career pain" that prompted their initiative to pursue a public forum, making known their desire to leave their profession.

In the days after the seminar, I had an opportunity to meet privately with many of the participants through individual career-counseling sessions. Over and over, I heard from these individuals that, at the time they chose to pursue law as a career, they really did not understand what the profession involved until they completed their schooling and became employed. Statements of this type are a common refrain among individuals who have chosen to pursue a number of occupations, not only law. A thorough lack of understanding of one's career options is commonplace.

You will enhance the quality of your career decision making by gaining a thorough understanding of what your options promise. The more you know about your options, the better you can determine the potential for each option to match your career profile. Good quality career information allows you to better evaluate your choices and to make more prudent plans for implementing your career decision.

This section of *Decision Time* describes sources for obtaining valuable career information. Additionally, recommendations are presented on the types of career information important for you to gather to better evaluate the career options you are considering.

Locating Career Information Resources

Many would-be career changers fall short of making a change because of the uncertainty associated with pursuing a new career option. Many times clients have told me, "If only there was a way to know [that the career decision I am contemplating will result in a positive outcome]." Unfortunately, there is no way to "know" whether or not any career option you are considering will prove right for you. You can, however, hedge your chances of selecting the best available choice by empowering yourself with as much good-quality information as possible. Good career information allows you to reduce the uncertainty associated with decision making, be more discriminating in evaluating your options, and be more confident in your decision making. First, you need to know where to look to find this information.

Since *Decision Time* was first published in 1994, the Internet and available computer-based resources have evolved phenomenally. Rich and expansive sources of career information are literally available at your fingertips.

Many public and private organizations maintain Web sites that can be rich sources of career information. Perusing these Web sites can give you a wide range of information – from insight about the organization's culture, business trends and objectives, to key personnel. Many organizations list pending job opportunities on their Web site.

Other Internet-based information I recommend you consider includes Web sites maintained by trade and professional associations, job banks, and want ads published by newspapers in various locales. Also, consider visiting Web sites of newspapers such as *USA Today*. This Web site includes an excellent career section on topics such as developing your resume, earnings and job outlooks, interviewing and networking, and researching prospective employers. This site also has a "post a resume" service, and has featured other interactive services such as allowing readers to pose specific career questions which, in turn, are answered by professional career counselors.

Appendix C includes a list of Web sites to start your quest for career information. The Web sites are categorized as career research, company research, finding jobs, career advice, salary information, networking information, general search engines, and additional Web sites. I also recommend that you visit Web sites such as careerbuilder.com. This Web site features articles on resume writing, developing cover letters, job finding, networking, interviewing and negotiating job offers, changing careers, jobs and the economy, managing your career, and general workplace issues. I recently visited this resource and was intrigued by topics such as "Overqualified? How to adjust your resume," "12 steps to surviving unemployment," "Inventive tactics to land a job," "Lying on your resume: Why it doesn't pay," "Fitting in with office misfits," and "18 ways to impress your employer."

Another good source of career information is a local library. A good reference section contains both general and specific career information on labor market trends and specific occupations and industries, as well as local and national career-related information.

Your local chamber of commerce or the one in the area where you are considering pursuing your career development can also provide rich career information. Profiles of emerging industries and employers, listings of major employers within an area, and trends within the business community are the types of information a chamber of commerce can provide. To get the most out of this type of research, I recommend you identify committees that interest you within the chamber of commerce – such as international trade, relocation, or women-owned businesses – and actively participate. This will enable you to learn about career development opportunities from those who are driving your local business community.

Another good source of career information is a trade or professional association. Many professional associations conduct surveys of their membership. These surveys often provide information about salary levels of individuals within the profession, demographic breakdowns, credentials and experience levels of those within the profession, and types of industries employing its members. Additionally, many professional associations have local chapters that can provide you with further networking opportunities.

Government-generated career information is also valuable. There are several publications, many of which are available online, from the U.S. Department of Labor that are truly outstanding. Among these are the *Occupational Outlook Handbook*, a biannual publication that identifies a wealth of current career information including descriptive information about occupations, education, and training requirements, salary information, and projections on labor market trends.

Another Department of Labor publication, *The Guide for Occupational Exploration*, lists occupations by groups of related families; this resource is particularly useful for exploring how skills you have already developed could be transferred to alternate occupations and career paths. *The Enhanced Guide for Occupational Exploration* is better-suited for those who want more detailed information about job responsibilities associated with common jobs.

The *Occupational Outlook Quarterly* is another fine Department of Labor publication. This periodical has information on career trends, emerging career areas, and timely information on issues such as occupations projected to be in high demand as well as those that are projected to be on the decline, and rankings of occupations by earnings level. A recent article, for example, listed the highest paying occupations that do not require a high school diploma. And what is the highest paying occupation without a diploma? You are correct if you guessed bail bonding agent.

At the state government level, your state's Department of Labor can provide even more detailed information specific to metropolitan areas throughout your state. Employer-specific information can also be obtained through this source.

Many computer-based guidance systems include excellent repositories of career information. Some of these systems are available in career centers at community colleges, universities, libraries, and even in some business and government organizations. The information that can be accessed through the technology varies. Most of these systems include lists of occupations that are cross-referenced by variables such as earnings, training requirements, geographical location, projections on labor market demands, skills necessary to perform occupations and, in some cases, personality traits associated with successful job incumbents. Reference librarians and counselors can help you make optimal use of this technology.

An often overlooked source of career information is interviewing people who actually hold positions that interest you. Why not get the scoop on a career that you are considering from someone who has already embarked in the career? You may be surprised at how much you can learn and the amount of goodwill you can build for the cost of a lunch. Informational interviews offer a human perspective and provide far richer data for you to consider than any facts or statistics publications can offer.

A qualified career counselor can also provide you with useful career information. At the very least, a career counselor should direct you to sources that may be unknown to you. The National Career Development Association can help you identify career counselors available in your locale; you can contact the organization toll free at (866) FOR-NCDA.

Many career counselors administer standardized vocational tests that can be useful in your subsequent research. Depending on the tests, you can obtain information about various personal and career-related aspects of yourself in relation to different career choices. If you are a college graduate, consult your alumni office about career-related services that may be available to you. Local community colleges may also offer these types of services.

You can obtain further career information through various community-based sources such as employment services offered through the private and public sectors, courses and seminars offered through local educational institutions, and services offered through faith-based organizations.

One caution about occupational information is that it can quickly become obsolete. There is an abundance of good-quality, current career information. Your research efforts will ideally combine the sources previously listed to help you learn as much as possible about each of your options. Appendix D lists people resources for you to consult in your research efforts. A bibliography of print materials that provides career information is in Appendix E. Besides consulting these sources, you can learn about the options you are considering through volunteer work related to your career choice. Sometimes you can acquire information through part-time work related to the options you are considering. Whatever methods you choose, it behooves you to consult every possible source available so you can better understand your choices.

Gathering the Right Information: What Do I Need to Know?

A particularly interesting research study on the topic of career choice in which I was involved at the University of South Florida examined how college students became committed to their choice of a college major. The research question was "What are the primary influences on how college students select and commit to their choice of a college major?" The most frequent influences that students cited were role models. Parents, teachers, neighbors, relatives, athletic coaches – all contribute to the popularity of this category. The second strongest influence on these students' choice of a college major, however, was surprising if not alarming: television.

Much of what we learn about the world, including the world of work, comes to us through the media. Unfortunately, the images of work portrayed through television and media are often incomplete and only partially accurate. This can lead people to form stereotypes about various occupations.

We sometimes form an image of an occupation based solely on its title. Consider, for example, the following occupational titles and the image that your mind conjures: Investment Banker. Contractor. Psychologist. High School Teacher. Accountant. Computer Programmer. Pharmacist.

I am trying to make two main points through this discussion. First, many of our notions about various career options are formed through inaccurate stereotypes that we cultivate during our lifetimes. Second, these stereotypes may cause us to prejudge and eliminate legitimate occupations from our consideration.

The depth of information you gather from the several exercises outlined in this section will help you to examine the "fit" between your work priorities, interests, skills and aptitudes, personal factors, and your career options. The information that you gather will be enriched to the extent that it addresses these personal matters. For instance, if your career decision boils down to a choice between accepting one of two equally attractive job opportunities, your ability to learn supervisory styles of each prospective employer could cast a significant amount of weight in your final analysis.

While digging deeply in your research is important, you must also be prudent. We can overdo anything, including analyzing our options to the point that we find ourselves in a "paralysis by analysis" mode. As in many other situations, the Pareto Principle is a good guide to observe when conducting your career research: If you have gathered 80% of the information required to make a decision, go ahead and make your decision. The remaining 20% of the information will probably not significantly add to the quality of your decision.

Depending on the nature of your career decision and your options, the information you require will, of course, differ. If you are considering self-employment or starting up a business, for example, you will need information about venture capital, market share held by competitors, and consumer patterns and trends. The most common career information needs include education and training opportunities, specific occupational industry areas, and specific employers. Suggestions on the precise information to gather for each of these categories follow.

Education and Training Opportunities

Early during the course of my work with a client, I try to determine how the client views pursuing additional education and training. Some wish to use the skills they have already developed in exploring their options. Others may have a strong desire or need to pursue significant retraining. Individuals whose jobs have been eliminated, often because their jobs have been modified by technology – dislocated workers – are a prime example. Honestly addressing the question of additional education and retraining as it relates to your career plans is essential. Virtually every career change will be accompanied by a learning curve that will require a period for you to develop your skills to a level that will make you competitive in the labor market.

From my experience as a private-practice career counselor and organizational consultant, less than half of those with whom I have worked have pursued significant retraining. A career change is not necessarily synonymous with retraining. Many individuals strategically transfer the skills they have already developed and expand their career opportunities through on-the-job training, self-study, or participation in selected learning opportunities. For others, education and training programs that last from several weeks to six months can sometimes unveil a range of new opportunities. Many career changers choose to return to a formal education setting and pursue certificate programs or academic degrees.

Besides the traditional model of learning offered by educational institutions in which students enroll in classes they attend on a campus at specified dates and times on a set schedule, keep in mind that many educational institutions offer alternate formats such as weekend programs and distance learning. These alternatives are particularly attractive to those who have special flexibility and accessibility needs.

Distance learning, which involves learning through formats such as television broadcasting and the Internet, can be a convenient way for people with accessibility problems to avail themselves to learning opportunities. Many individuals with disabilities and individuals who live in remote areas, for example, can benefit from distance learning. Information about distance learning opportunities can be obtained by reviewing Web sites of institutions that interest you or by contacting admissions officers at those institutions. Also offered online are courses from vendors of products such as personal digital assistants and digital cameras.

Apart from educational institutions, there are many other sources that provide opportunities to develop new skills that can help you to expand your career choices. Most mid-size and large businesses and nonprofit organizations, for example, have a training department that offers professional development programs for its employees. Educational programs offered through professional associations, private training firms, and community-based training programs are other sources where you can refine existing skills and develop new skills. There is also a growing selection of self-directed professional-development resources – books, audiotapes, CDs, and computer programs – on topics ranging from developing foreign language skills to learning to operate specialized software. Opportunities to develop your skills in any imaginable area abound.

Before you commit to any formal education or training program, I recommend you first thoroughly research the program before you commit time, energy, or money. I have, unfortunately, encountered situations in which clients apprised me of time consuming, expensive training programs they completed – only to learn the program was not accredited as represented. Also, I have encountered situations in which clients were disappointed at the completion of a training program when they learned the credentialing they attained did not unlock the types of career options they hoped to be able to pursue.

It is best to first speak directly with the department head, senior faculty member, or placement officer for information about the employment of graduates from the institutions you are considering for education/training. I recommend that you ask the following questions:

> *Tell me about your last class of graduates. What types of positions did they secure? What types of organizations are they working in today? What help did your institution provide in helping these graduates find their jobs? What was the average salary level the graduates attained? Can I have the names of two or three of your alumni to gain their perspectives on your program?*

Many of my clients find that some of their more appealing options require further training. Sometimes they become disappointed and dissuaded because the amount of training required appears overwhelming and they are apprehensive about the associated time, lifestyle adjustment, and financial commitments. The biggest objections typically relate to the loss of earnings while pursuing additional training and the actual cost associated with the training. I believe that if an individual is willing to make the sacrifices associated with retraining, finding the money to fund the endeavor will not stand in the way. A loan, employer-subsidized training, scholarships, personal funds – all are means to finance education and retraining costs. The real question is whether the individual is willing to make necessary lifestyle adjustments.

If you are considering further education or training, I recommend that you consider the following before you make your commitment:

- Benefits that graduates of the program have attained.
- Training provided, including program curriculum and training methods used.
- Career paths of individuals who have completed the training.
- Credits for past education and also for work experiences.
- Admissions criteria and characteristics of other training participants .
- Costs, payment methods, alternatives for subsidizing training expenses.
- Interest, compatibility of values, lifestyle and abilities.
- Motivation – can it be sustained?

Specific Occupations or Industries

If a career option you are considering is outside your current career field or industry you should seriously study your options lest you risk the chance of trial-and-error career development, which I described earlier. I have included a bibliography of print materials in Appendix E to facilitate your research.

Although I recommend you read about your options, hands-on insight into your prospective new career field or industry also has value. Some of the most effective methods of this type of research involve conducting informational interviews with those who are already working within an occupation or industry that appeals to you. An informational interview is different from a job interview in that you are interviewing someone to learn more about a career path that you are considering, rather than interviewing as a job candidate for a specific position. In most cases, those you approach will be accommodating – even though they may not know you. I have found that most people are flattered when others show interest in their work and, accordingly, their pride leads them to want to describe their occupations with those who express interest.

When approaching someone for an informational interview, I recommend that you request a 15- to 20-minute meeting. Be sure to keep it to that and be sure to thank the person for the courtesy. One of my clients who is particularly skilled in informational interviewing managed to land an attractive job through an informational interview after she learned about a specific interest her future boss had in computer networking systems. She took the initiative to research the latest trends in this area and briefed the future employer, who was so impressed he created a position for her.

Getting an inside perspective can sometimes provide far more information than you can ever gain from written sources. Those who are most effective in conducting information interviews not only learn what an average day on the job is like, they learn how those who have been most effective have moved ahead. These insights can prove invaluable as you plan and manage your career development.

One of the best ways to gain information about a career path or industry is to do what career counselors refer to as "reality testing." This involves actually performing work or working in an environment in the career path to which you aspire before you make the commitment to pursue your new option. Some of the most common methods of reality testing include "shadowing" or watching someone perform the work that you are interested in, volunteering for similar work in the field, participating in part-time work, or taking a trial assignment in an area that interests you.

As you proceed with your research, I recommend that you specifically seek the following information:

- Wage and salary information
- Labor force projections
- Hiring and promotion patterns
- Credentials required
- Types of employers and work settings
- Career paths available after entering a field
- Working conditions
- Characteristics of entry-level and advanced positions
- Sensitivity of the field to economic, technological, and social forces
- Trends in the field
- Lifestyle implications associated with working in different positions within the field, including travel, stress, relocation, and advancement opportunities.

Prepare specific questions that address concerns you may have. Also, gaining the perspectives of several people would be helpful as you conduct this research.

Employer History

As you research various career fields and industries, you will likely encounter information about specific employers. Also, your research will probably pique your interest about employers who offer career development opportunities that are compatible with your interests. If your career decision ultimately involves a job search, you should carefully study the employers that could provide you with a good career opportunity, not just in the short term, but in your future career development as well. Again, I recommend that you consult Web sites posted by various organizations and employ other research means discussed in this book to help you find the information you need to enhance your analysis.

For large public organizations, and some nonprofit organizations, you can consult an annual report to learn about the employer. Annual reports can be easily obtained from the organization's public affairs department. Most placement offices at universities and colleges maintain a library of annual reports and recruiting literature from organizations that conduct on-campus interviews. Stockbrokers are another source for obtaining annual reports. Also, talk with employees of the organizations that you are researching.

The following list suggests useful career information to gather about prospective employers:

- Characteristics of prospective supervisors and coworkers
- Compensation and benefits
- Hiring and advancement prospects
- History, status, and long- and short-term goals of the organization
- How performance reviews are conducted
- Lifestyle demands such as long hours, frequent travel, and expectation to be relocated
- Management and supervisory styles
- Number of employees and location of offices
- Organizational chart showing the chain of command and potential career paths
- Organizational markets, products, services, sales, and profits
- Organizational philosophy, dynamics, culture, and politics
- Position descriptions and specifications
- Traditional career paths
- Training and development opportunities within the organization

Much of the information you gather will likely be from the Internet, but be aware of resources that can help you evaluate the quality of this information. The National Career Development Association (NCDA) has a Web site with guidelines about using the Internet to search for career information and planning at www.ncda.org. Appendix C also identifies Internet resources for career development. Many college and university career centers, like the Career Center at Florida State University, have Web sites with topics that range from effective Internet use to exploring education options and career information. I recommend that you consult these types of resources to help you gather and critically evaluate career-related information.

Getting Started

Well-researched career information allows you to explore your options further before you commit to a career change. This information is invaluable to your analysis and assessment of your options. Also, it helps you minimize uncertainty and risk, make prudent decisions and plans, and confidently move ahead in your career development. Besides knowing what information to obtain, it also helps to know what activities will enable you to discover information you require.

Several recommended information gathering activities follow. Regardless of whether you employ these activities or others, be sure to pursue activities most likely to help you uncover critical career information pertinent to your decision making and planning.

1. Begin with your computer or one available to you at a library or other source. Appendix C identifies many categorically organized Web sites to help guide your research. You will find that many Web sites have links to other helpful, vast amounts of information. Most people find their computer to be an important tool throughout the career decision-making and planning process. Allocate 1 or 2 hours per day to computer-based research during the information gathering of your career decision making.

2. Visit a good library in your locale – either a public library or one associated with an academic institution. You will be surprised at the vast collection of career-related resources available. The reference librarians can also be quite helpful, as they are trained professionals in finding very specific information. Ask for help!

3. As previously discussed, most people welcome the chance to help others in their career development. Identify two or three people who have established themselves in positions that you are considering. Membership lists, such as those composed by professional and trade organizations, faith-based organizations, and country clubs, are useful in identifying potential contacts. You can also identify potential contacts by reading the newspaper and other local publications that identify those active in your locale. Be sure to inform these individuals about your purpose for requesting an informational interview. During your interview, ask questions that will help you to learn how these individuals (a) attained their career positions, (b) dealt with the challenges they encountered during their career development, (c) spend an average day at their jobs, (d) would plan their career development in their field today, and (e) would advise you in your career decision. Before your interviews, prepare your questions, which may include *How did you get started in the field? What is your typical day like? What are the benefits and drawbacks of working in the field?*

4. Identify trade or professional associations within the career areas you are considering. Again, a reference librarian or a source at your local Chamber of Commerce can help you find this information. Contact the state or national office of a trade or professional association to obtain specific information. Also, if there is a local chapter of the organization within your community plan to attend a meeting. Better yet, volunteer your time and get involved on a committee that will help you to meet and network with people who are established within a career field that you care considering.

5. Visit a career center at a local college or university. These centers usually include a vast amount of print and computer-based resources to facilitate your career exploration and to provide information on various career fields. Some career centers also have recruiting information provided by prospective employers.

6. Contact your state's Department of Labor for current and specific information related to wages, job availability, and labor market projections for various occupations in major metropolitan areas.

7. Go to a bookstore and browse through titles of career-related books. Your knowledge, insight, and confidence will grow as you become better informed. Be mindful, however, of the Pareto Principle discussed earlier – you only need 80% of the information to make a decision.

8. Call your Chamber of Commerce to learn about various career-related resources it publishes. Again, become active in groups and committees that will allow you to network with others and obtain information that is otherwise unavailable. Your involvement in a committee or group can help you become more aware of a specific area and may help you to meet others who share your career interests.

Chapter 5

Taking Action

Taking Action

This chapter builds on your previous work that has included looking within yourself and researching information necessary to help you better understand your options. Specifically, we will focus on integrating this information as you continue to commit to your career decision and planning strategy.

To this point, while engaging in self-exploration activities and conducting research – there has been a degree of safety, perhaps even intrigue, in the process. I have found that many people have difficulty moving to the next step in the career decision-making process: committing to a decision and implementing the necessary steps to move ahead. My reminder to those who grow weary or timid when the time comes to move ahead and commit to a career decision is to reassess current levels of career fulfillment and to consider the enhancements your options promise. Or, as a colleague put it more directly, "If your career hasn't lived up to your expectations, take stock and do what it takes to get things back on track."

Any apprehension you may have over committing to and acting on a career decision is understandable. Few decisions we make during our lives have the magnitude of a career decision. As I discussed earlier in *Decision Time*, the work we perform on a daily basis truly touches all aspects of our lives. If you still do not feel comfortable moving ahead and committing to a career direction, you may want to consider consulting a professional career counselor. The perspective of a trained professional could provide the impetus needed to free you from the inertia hindering you from taking the action necessary to propel your career development.

In the decision-making and planning phases of the model I outlined earlier, you will work through the following steps:

- Integrate what you learned from looking within yourself along with the research you have gathered from your information gathering activities.

- Evaluate the "fit" between the career identify that emerged from your self-analysis and the options you are considering. Refer to your self-assessment summary sheet on page 64. Do you have the personal qualities and assets to meet the demands and requirements of your newly chosen career? What's missing and how can you get it?

- Commit to a career decision and set goals to help you get started on carry out your decision.

- Draft a career plan to help you think through how you will attain your goals.

There is no "correct" way to go about making a career decision that will guarantee positive outcomes. You can, however, improve your chances of success by carefully following the five decision making steps described in Figure 11. This diagram presents an overview of the process.

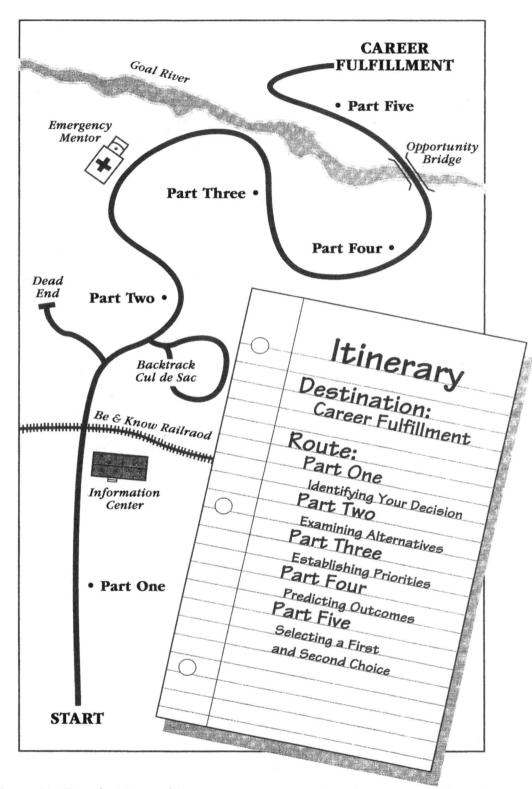

Figure 11. Five decision-making steps to career action planning. Recycling through this process will help you keep your career development on track.

No two people approach their career decisions the same way. Having a structure, however, to guide your decision making will ensure that you have carefully examined the vital aspects of your decision. Because of such factors as our experiences, risk-taking propensity, personality traits, self-confidence, available financial and support resources, and our career identities, we all have different influences and styles that affect our decision making.

Identifying Your Decision

What are some of the more common career decisions we confront?

- Making an occupational change

- Pursuing an entrepreneurial track by either starting-up a business, buying an existing business, forming a partnership, or buying into a franchise

- Accepting or declining a job offer or promotion

- Deciding to stay where you are in your career path

- Choosing to invest in your self-development by pursuing additional education or training

- Deciding to retrench from the workforce through reduced hours, part-time work, or semiretirement

- Choosing among different job offers that may have been extended

- Returning to the workforce after a period of absence

- Committing to a new career field

- Deciding to transfer some of your energy and focus away from your career and into other activities such as volunteer work and leisure or social pursuits

In as much detail as possible, use the following space to write and describe your pending career decisions and the implications associated with your decisions. You will find this helpful in focusing on the driving forces behind your decision making. In particular, consider the six journalistic questions as you write out the career decision you face: *Who* is involved in my career decision? *What* are the key issues in my decision? *Where* do I want to focus my future career development? *Why* am I considering a career change? *When* do I plan to make my change? *How* am I proposing to go about making my change.

_____

_____

_____

_____

Career Decision

_____

_____

_____

_____

_____

_____

_____

_____

_____

_____

_____

_____

_____

_____

_____

_____

_____

_____

_____

_____

_____

_____

_____

_____

_____

_____

Examining Alternatives

By definition, a decision requires that you have two or more options under consideration. When examining your alternatives, having side-by-side criteria related to your analysis is helpful.

To compare your options fairly, I recommend that you consider each option in relation the following points:

- Positive Characteristics – What attracts you to this option?

- Negative Characteristics – What about this option causes you concern?

- Degree of Risk – How much risk is associated with choosing this option? Is this level of risk acceptable to you

- Feasibility – How doable is this option? Given your present situation, is it a realistic option at this time?

- Resources Required – Some people are fortunate to possess career-related resources such as the support of your boss, coworkers, family, and friends; the necessary education, experience, training and credentials; the time to pursue a new career path; and, sometimes, having the necessary financial resources. As you examine the resources to you, do you find your career-related resources sufficient to pursue the career options you are considering?

- Your Willingness to Commit – Along with the risk involved in changing careers, a certain degree of energy on your part is required to make the change. Additionally, if you can change careers, you must also be willing to accept the uncertainty that goes along with any transition. Too much ambivalence can thwart a good plan and strategy. As you ponder these issues, how willing are you to commit to the various career options you are considering?

Through my research, I have found that reducing your career decision to two or three options is more effective than entertaining too many career choices. The worksheet entitled "Evaluating Career Options" (Figure 12) will help you make a side-by-side comparison of the career options you are evaluating. First, write out your career decision in the space at the top of the worksheet.

Then, list each option you are considering on the left side of the worksheet. Next, use the headings on the worksheet to guide your thinking about the key aspects associated with your career options. Write your reactions in the spaces provided on the worksheet. The last heading, "Other Factors" is where you comment on significant factors that have not already been addressed.

Figure 12. Evaluating Career Options

EVALUATING CAREER OPTIONS

Career Decision _____

Options	Positive Characteristics	Negative Characteristics	Degree of Risk	Feasibility	Sufficiency of Resources	Your Willingness to commit	Other Factors
Option 1							
Option 2							
Option 3							

Establishing Priorities

There are many ways to prioritize your career options. Some people relate well to a ranking method in which they weigh different aspects of their options on a 1-to-10 scale, with a 1 indicating the low end of the scale and 10 indicating the high end. Other people rely more on subjective factors to help them establish priorities – what their instincts tell them, what feels right, or what seems to make sense. Still others find it useful to speak to people whose opinion they respect and trust. I recommend you use all of these methods.

First, go back to the worksheet on the preceding pages. Review what you have written with your analysis of the options you are considering. After your review, assign each option a ranking, based on the 1-to-10 scale referenced above.

Second, reexamine your responses on the worksheet. This time approach your analysis more from a feeling perspective. That is, how does each of the options appeal to your sense of what feels like a good match for you?

Third, consult two people whom you believe are well qualified to review the information you provided on the worksheet and to provide candid insight and guidance into your career decision making. A mentor, trusted colleague, significant other, and counselor are people you may want to consult. Ask their opinions about your evaluation of the key aspects related to your decision.

The chart in Figure 13 will help you consolidate your perspectives about your options. Again, summarize this information in the space provided for your future reference.

Figure 13. Prioritizing Options

	Ranking of Options (1 to 10 Scale)	Feelings About My Options	Opinions of Those I Consulted With
Option 1			
Option 2			
Option 3			

Predicting Outcomes

Every quality career decision includes earnestly deliberating your potential for success. Predicting the likelihood of success and attaining your career goals *before* you commit to a new direction is essential. Unless your career decision is tempered with reality, you risk taking your career development down a time-consuming path of frustration.

Again, there is no sure way to predict the outcome of the career decisions you make. Sometimes people become dissuaded from pursuing a career decision because, for example, they have learned through their research that the labor market demand for an occupation they may be considering is not favorable. While information of this type is important, the will and commitment within a person is perhaps more important in predicting one's changes for success than positive or negative labor market projections. One of my favorite examples involves a colleague who went against the prevailing wisdom and committed to fulfilling his goal of earning an MBA degree and becoming a lecturer at a major university – despite contracting Lou Gehrig's disease. He incurred a series of progressive physical limitations that left him paralyzed below the neck and dependent upon a ventilator. His family and friends discouraged him from leaving the advertising firm where, after 21 years, he had worked his way up to a partnership, security, and a competitive salary. Not only was he successful in accomplishing his career goals, he published two books related to his newly developed area of expertise: *mass communications for people with disabilities.*

Predicting your chances for success in whatever option you ultimately choose involves both objective and subjective processes. Your estimate of your ability to successfully attain various options you are considering depends upon both the thoroughness in which you approach your exploration of your career identify and the research you conduct on your options.

Perhaps the most effective way to hedge your bets on a choice before you commit to it is to outline a plan to implement each career decision you are seriously considering. In some ways, I think of a career plan as a piece of Swiss cheese: both are firm and have a definite shape, yet both are filled with holes. Architects draw blueprints, athletic coaches form game plans, business people develop business plans, and writers create outlines to guide their work before they embark on it. It makes sense that you develop your own career plan to help you design and manage your career development. Like almost every type of work product, the quality of the final outcome often depends upon the planning before the actual work has begun. The better your planning, the fewer the holes in your plans.

A good career plan helps you convert your aspirations to outcomes. And your chances for success grow along with the quality of your career plan.

Successful career plans share three common features: *Specificity, Realism,* and *Flexibility.* In terms of specificity, your career plan should contain details. It should also be realistic in terms of what you can attain in a reasonable period. Finally, your career plan should be flexible and allow for adjustments and refinements to accommodate unforseen changes that will certainly arise as you undertake various actions to convert your plans to outcomes.

Depending on your career objectives, details relevant to your career planning will vary. For example, if your ultimate objective is to assume a more responsible position in your current occupation or field – an objective that may require additional training, experience, and eventually employment in a different organization – your career plan will address different planning issues than someone whose objective is starting a new business. This latter objective would likely require the planning of financial, marketing, operations management, and other related details.

While career plans differ in terms of the information they contain, they are similar in structure. Effective career plans address the following details:

- *Short Term Goals* – Those you hope to attain within the next 3 to 12 months.

- *Long Term Goals* – Objectives you hope to attain within the next 1 to 3 years.

- *Steps Necessary to Achieve Goals* – Details on each of the career milestones necessary for you to accomplish to move closer to your long-term career goals.

- *Strategy* – How you achieve your career objectives.

- *Necessary Resources* – As discussed earlier, these will probably vary depending upon your career decision and might include things such as additional training, capital for the start-up of a new business venture, or possibly support from your boss or family members.

- *Projected Time Frame* – A successful career plan outlines realistic dates for achieving each career milestone.

- *Criteria for Evaluating Your Success* – As you progress toward your career goals, having preestablished criteria to monitor your progress is useful.

- *Back-up Plan* – Just in case: What plans do you have if your efforts are unsuccessful?

Of course, identifying the near-term steps to move forward in your career development is easier than identifying the longer-term steps. Because many variables and assumptions are subject to change, drafting a complete career plan is impossible. When drafting your career plan, try to identify as many intermediate steps as possible that are necessary to move ahead. Thinking of what your future resume might look like if you have accomplished your objectives may be helpful.

Figure 14 on the following pages includes a Career Plan Worksheet for your use in thinking and working through the many planning details associated with your career options. As you complete your career plan, keep in mind the three essential elements common to successful career plans: *Specificity, Realism,* and *Flexibility.* In as much detail as possible, write out your plan for moving ahead with the top three options you are considering.

Figure 14.

CAREER PLAN WORKSHEET

First Choice:
Short-term goals: _____
Long-term goals: _____

Action Strategy	Essential Resources	Projected Starting Date	Projected Completion Date	Criteria for Evaluating Success	Back-up Plan

Second Choice:
Short-term goals: _____
Long-term goals: _____

Action Strategy	Essential Resources	Projected Starting Date	Projected Completion Date	Criteria for Evaluating Success	Back-up Plan

Third Choice:
Short-term goals: _____
Long-term goals: _____

Action Strategy	Essential Resources	Projected Starting Date	Projected Completion Date	Criteria for Evaluating Success	Back-up Plan

Making the Commitment

At this point in your decision-making process, you have expended a great deal of time and energy looking within yourself, researching your options, and proceeding to systematically make a career decision. The most difficult parts of the process, however, are making the commitment to move forward and taking the necessary actions to implement your decision.

If you have worked through the recommended activities presented in *Decision Time*, you undoubtedly will have more confidence in proceeding with your decision. Ideally, at least one of the options you identified truly excites you.

Perhaps the best way to make a commitment to a career decision and to hold true to it is to enlist the help of others. In a later section of *Decision Time* I will discuss the value of cultivating a strong relationship with a mentor.

We eventually reach a point where, as the phrase goes, we must "Just do it." The following ideas may help keep you on task:

- Regularly review your objectives and career plan. Some clients find it helpful to post a photocopy of their career plans in a visible place to remind them of their objectives.

- Enlist the support of one or two trusted individuals, and ask that they periodically prompt and coach you on moving forward.

- Make conscious efforts to engage the target actions outlined on your career plan. Focus on the benefits these behaviors will allow you to realize. Also, some find it helpful to establish contingencies to reward themselves when they have attained various milestones en route to their career objectives. Treat yourself to a dinner out after you have taken your first major step toward implementing your career decision.

Recommended Implementation Activities

Below are some activities to help you implement your career plan.

1. Outline below specific activities you can initiate within the next 30 days.

2. Identify two or three people whom you trust and know can be helpful in implementing your career objectives. Write their names below, and describe what you will do to involve them in your career planning activities.

3. List all reasons you have for not moving forward in your career development. Discuss these reasons with the people you identified above, and make any necessary fine tuning changes to your career plan. Again, this may be the time you choose to seek professional guidance from a career counselor.

Chapter 6

Fine-Tuning Your
Career Strategy

Fine-Tuning Your Career Strategy

From time to time we have all wondered, "What does it take to get ahead? How can I accelerate the pace of my career development?" This chapter presents my observations, gleaned from more than 20 years of practice as a career counselor helping individuals from nearly all walks of life. Fourteen factors that I have found correlated with career success are described. Incorporating these factors in a positive way can enable you to break through plateaus in your career development and realize your true career potential.

None of the 14 factors will guarantee your career success; however, many are vital. The Career Management Survey (Figure 15) provides an opportunity to inventory your career management assets. Your candid responses to the questions will help you better identify how to positively manage your career.

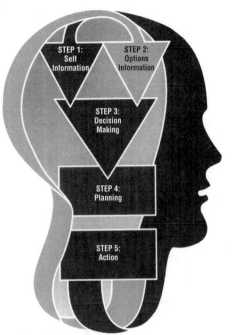

Career Management Tip #1
Lineage: Use It If You've Got It – Get It If You Don't

Without question, one of the biggest boosts to your career development is to have the good fortune of coming from a family background steeped in a history of success in business and community service affairs. Look at the most influential business people in your community. My bet is that many are from old-line, prominent families with histories of success in business and contributions to community service. Often, family power has been handed down from generation to generation, and the family name has become an institution within the community.

If you are fortunate to have this type of career advantage, my advice is to use it – but use it with caution. Nothing can be a bigger turn-off than someone who is arrogant and boorish, trying to ride the coat tails of their family's fame and fortune. The key to leveraging the legacy of your family's success in your career development is your grace and skill in using it. You can never have enough allies in your career development; however, developing relationships that are not vested in helping you meet your career objectives is possible.

Having the type of family lineage and influence that can attract people's attention, get phone calls returned that might not otherwise be returned, and gain introductions to key decision makers is helpful. A solid network of influential contacts can help you to develop a lineage, and I recommend that you attempt to do this. Few of us are born into this advantage or have it readily available, however, so keep reading.

Career Management Tip #2
Confidence: Don't Go Into the Workplace Without It

If you believe in yourself, if you are truly committed to a career direction and putting forth the necessary effort to take your career to the next plateau, my bet is that you will be successful in your career development. Without a true belief in yourself, however, your career prospects will be severely limited, and you will probably not realize your potential; it is as predictable as that.

The Career Management Survey

For each of the statements below, check either T for True or F for False.

	T	F
1. I consider my family's background and my network of contacts, in terms of their influence in my business community, to be an asset to my career development.	___	___
2. I have a strong self-concept, and I am confident that I will develop a successful career.	___	___
3. My career direction is unfocused. That is, I am unclear about how my work values, interests, skills and aptitudes, and personality traits relate to my career direction.	___	___
4. When it comes to taking risks in my career, I become very apprehensive.	___	___
5. I have yet to develop a significant presence within either my profession or my business community.	___	___
6. My lack of motivation, desire, and drive to advance my career development has concerned me.	___	___
7. I have a mentor who is an asset to my career development.	___	___
8. I am confident that the competence and skills I possess are more than adequate for me to be successful in my career development.	___	___
9. I have sufficient resources (including financial resources and the support of my boss, mentor, colleagues, family and friends, employer, etc.) to support my career developments.	___	___
10. I am good at marketing my career development; that is, doing the things that are necessary to get the attention of those with influence.	___	___
11. My life is well-balanced between career, relationships, leisure, community involvement, spirituality, physical health, and personal development.	___	___
12. I am good at "creating luck" — keeping active in finding opportunities to be in the right places at the right times.	___	___
13. Pride is a driving force in my career development.	___	___
14. I can use my power appropriately to advance my career objectives.	___	___

Confidence is an intangible, difficult-to-define characteristic. Surprisingly, we are sometimes the only ones who realize when it is low. On the other hand, sometimes a person's low self-esteem is evident. Lack of confidence can creep out and belie our presentation through our language, the way we present and carry ourselves nonverbally through our body language, our aspirations (or lack of aspirations), and the relationships we engage in – as well as those that we are too apprehensive to initiate. Warning signs of low self-esteem include settling for less than your best, excessive perfectionism, not valuing your work, and being uncomfortable with recognition.

If your self-concept is low and you lack a true belief in yourself, you owe it to yourself to invest in this aspect of your well being before you proceed with your career development. Seek out a trusted friend or perhaps a professional counselor to help you understand the reasons for your self-perception. If you do not value the work you do, how can you value yourself for doing it? A healthy self-concept and firm belief in yourself is paramount to developing a successful career. I cannot overstate the importance of a healthy self-concept and the confidence that it generates. This confidence is essential to allow you to take the risks necessary to advance your career development. Nevertheless, a less-than-desirable job situation can lower your self-worth.

Those with low self-esteem often have low career aspirations and, invariably, underachieve their career potential. A self-fulfilling prophesy typically occurs. Because the individual has little self-confidence, he or she sets low career objectives to avoid risk and potential failure. Less than stellar career progress, in turn, reinforces low expectations for career success. The self-fulfilling prophesy is reinforced and, consequently, perpetuated.

I could offer countless examples of clients who have had very low self-concepts that, almost unknown to them, had devastating effects on their career development. Perhaps the best example is that of a teacher in her mid 30s. Teaching had been her lifetime vocation. I counseled her in my practice for several months after she had unequivocally expressed her dissatisfaction with her career as an eighth-grade English teacher. After completing several vocational tests and counseling sessions, we identified many attractive, feasible career alternatives for her to pursue. Still, she was reluctant to initiate the change. I decided to try a different approach: I recommended that she pursue part-time work so that she could be exposed to career options outside a school setting and still regain momentum toward implementing her desired career change. She agreed, and I helped her gain an introduction to the personnel director of a major theme park in the area.

My client favorably impressed the personnel director during a job interview, and the director asked her which of the hundreds of different jobs in the theme park most appealed to her. The personnel director noted that job opportunities within the park were as diverse as feeding animals, serving in one of the many restaurants, working in a gift store, driving a monorail, and just about any other type of job associated with a large theme park. Her response, "I'd like to be the person who walks around the park and picks up the trash."

When she told me about her choice, I was – just as you probably are – astonished. I asked, "Why?" She offered sheepishly, "because I didn't want to disappoint him by not being able to do a job that he might offer me, so I chose something I knew I could handle."

My young client was projecting her low self-esteem into her career aspirations. This example shows, all too vividly, how a lack of self-confidence can place artificial ceilings on your career potential. How many of us set similar limits imposed by nothing more than our low self-esteem? Unfortunately, many people place limits on their career development that are simply a projection of their lack of self-esteem.

Confidence leads to taking risks, a necessity for accelerating your career development. If you do not have confidence in yourself, others probably will not either. This includes your boss, potential employers, colleagues, customers and clients, friends, peers, and family. Need I say more?

Career Management Tip #3
Focus: Set Your Sights and Go For It

Considering an important career decision is straightforward: know where you are going before you begin. Few people stumble their way to successful career development.

Getting to know yourself in a career, psychological, and personal sense is hard work – and the process never ends. While many people search for personal and career fulfillment, few invest the time and energy necessary to focus on themselves and their alternatives.

Earlier, I discussed how you can consolidate your career identity by examining your work values, interests, personality traits, and skills and aptitudes. I also highlighted the type of career information that is vital to help you gain a thorough understanding of your options so that you can decide about the appropriateness of your career choices. I think that our most difficult career decisions are the longer-term decisions. That is, where do you, ultimately, want to take your career? Too many people procrastinate when facing this decision because of its magnitude, fear of making the wrong decision, and the hard work that will inevitably be required to implement the decision. Once you have committed to the longer-term decision, you have, in effect, thrown out an anchor that, if used correctly, can guide your future decision making. From then on, your career decisions become more clear: Will the short-term decisions you face advance you to your ultimate career destination? Your decisions become straightforward once you put them in this perspective.

Most executives today are very savvy at detecting the commitment and sincerity people express and demonstrate toward their stated goals. Also, you can sense the intensity in people who have a true focus and desire to guide their career development. These individuals are in charge, intense, directed, and focused.

When you have a focus, you can better position yourself in places where attractive career opportunities will likely avail. You are also better able to spot opportunities as they arise so that you can take advantage of them. You will know that your focus is increasing when you approach your career goals with a passion.

Career Management Tip #4
Take Risks: You Can't Win If You Don't Play

If you want to attain more than a linear career development – that is, a traditional career development characterized by annual pay raises and predictable, periodic promotions – you must take risks. It is only through judicious risk taking that you can expedite your career development progress.

I am not suggesting that you go about randomly making high-risk decisions – like a novice investor placing a life savings into speculative, high-risk options in hope of a big payoff. Quite the contrary, I recommend that you take measured risks, after carefully discerning and developing opportunities through careering activities like volunteering for challenging projects that are beyond those you have already mastered, seeking new leadership opportunities, and daring to risk your time and ego by learning new skills and making the inevitable mistakes that go long with learning. You cannot afford to simply do a good job and then sit and wait, hoping someone will notice your talents and genius, and ultimately extend the break that you have been dreaming of to further your career development.

Too many people are overly conservative in their approach to career development. While they may be well focused and aware of opportunities they seek, they are sometimes too selective and move too slowly toward opportunities. Often, individuals wait for opportunities to avail in perfect form, but these types of opportunities rarely, if ever, occur. Others overanalyze opportunities. Then, when they are finally ready to act, the opportunity has gone. Do not wait passively on the sidelines for opportunities to arise in perfect form. Be a player, be bold, and carpe diem (seize the day).

Career Management Tip #5
Make Your Presence Known

An article in *Florida Trend*, a widely circulated business publication in the Southeast researched defining characteristics of the most successful business leaders from major metropolitan areas within the state. Specifically, the author's aim was to determine the most common correlates of business influence and power. The most common factor associated with these executives' success was their involvement in community and professional organizations.

Multitudes of professional, community, and social organizations provide outstanding opportunities to meet and interact with business leaders from various industries and organizations, both within your community and at a national or international level. I recommend that you start with considering your local chamber of commerce, trade and industry organizations, service clubs, charitable organizations, alumni organizations, and social groups. All offer outstanding opportunities for meeting and developing relationships with those who have knowledge and influence within your profession and community.

One of the biggest problems with executives who have fallen out of the grace of their employers is their lack of involvement in anything beyond their place of employment. These executives often become myopic within their organization. Their whole professional world, unfortunately, becomes limited to the place in which they work. Consequently, they fail to develop a network of outside contacts that could provide the link to the greater business community and, correspondingly, career development opportunities. When tough times come, they are often left standing alone, without a clue about how to resume their careers outside their organization. Without a network of colleagues to access, they resort to the resources of the masses: want ads and search firms.

Not only is volunteerism a charitable act that enables you to make meaningful contributions to your community and profession, your career development can greatly profit from your service. Through active involvement, you stand to gain visibility as a leader, meet and build community relationships with people of influence, and enhance your chances of being exposed to career advancement opportunities. Additionally, there are many self-development opportunities you can gain through volunteering. Chairing and serving on committees, interacting with individuals with common and diverse interests and expertise who can prove to be valuable business contacts, enhancing your existing skills and knowledge, and exposure to career opportunities – all are potential derivatives of a well-managed career plan that includes carefully selected volunteer activities.

My message to the prudent career planner: Be selective in committing to professional community organizations that can offer the greatest return to your career development, as well as those that can offer you a vehicle for making meaningful contributions to your profession and community. Don't overdo it, *but do it!*

Roll up your sleeves and get involved. Aim for high visibility, leadership opportunities that will accomplish the dual benefit of contributing to your community or profession while propelling your career prospects. A well-balanced career plan includes active involvement in professional and community organizations. Be more than a dues-paying paper member of the organizations with which you affiliate.

Career Management Tip #6
Drive: Put Passion Into Your Career

Call it motivation, desire, or hunger, but unless you have an internal drive for career success, your career development will plateau at a low level. Unmotivated and underachiever – labels nobody wants – are virtually symbiotic. Most worthwhile endeavors are accomplished with motivation and passion.

I sympathize with those who lack a strong work ethic and passion for the daily activities they undertake. Interestingly, many are from successful families. During my years in practice, I witnessed more cases than you might imagine: A 45-year-old journeyman real estate appraiser halfheartedly engaging his career while waiting for an inheritance from his wealthy father; a well-educated woman in her mid 30s, daughter of a prominent physician, who feels inadequate for not realizing her career potential, but greatly enjoys the hedonistic lifestyle afforded through her father's success; a middle-aged son of a successful entrepreneur, unjustifiably given an important position within his father's company that exceeds the limits of both his competence and ambition. While all of these people halfheartedly sought career counseling as a panacea for their lack of self-fulfillment, when push came to shove, they, like so many others devoid of internal motivation, stopped short of taking action and responsibility for their career development. Why? They lacked internal drive.

Some people can cultivate a strong internal drive by single-mindedly focusing on a career goal. Others are driven by competition; that is, the need to out-perform and exceed the accomplishments of either their peers or some identified standard. You will know if this passion is a part of you when you unconsciously find yourself doing things like taking on additional challenging assignments, working on airplanes while on personal or business travel in the absence of deadlines, and participating in activities that require sacrificing family and leisure time. This hunger for career success allows you to push yourself to new limits and set career goals that will take your career development to new heights. As the late Vince Lombardi, coach of the legendary championship Green Bay Packers football team so eloquently put it, "The difference between a successful person and others is not a lack of strength, not a lack of knowledge, but rather a lack of will."

Career Management Tip #7
Find a Mentor: A Guide Can Help You Find a Way

A recent survey of more than 1,200 top executives from the nation's largest companies found that approximately two-thirds of these executives had informal mentors or sponsors at some point during their careers. In 70% of the cases, the mentoring relationships began during the first 5 years of the executives' careers, and more than 25% indicated they later became mentors during the second decade of their careers. Generally, the survey reported that executives who have had a mentor earned more money at a younger age, are better educated, are more likely to follow a career path, and sponsor more proteges than executives who have not had a mentor.

The potential benefits of developing a strong relationship with a supportive mentor – who is truly interested in your career development – are obvious: someone who can share the wisdom gained from struggling with, and ultimately surmounting obstacles in his or her own career development; someone who can counsel you on critical decisions in your career development and remain available as a source of support and guidance; someone who can provide introductions and help to open doors to opportunities that you may be unable to open alone.

Ideally, your mentor should be someone who is at least two or more levels higher than your current level of career development. A good mentor can come from within or outside your organization. Be selective of the mentorship relationship that you cultivate. Whenever you can, of course, reciprocate the goodwill your mentor has extended to you – both to your mentor and to others. This includes acting as a mentor for others and helping to develop proteges who have yet to attain your level of career success. Your proteges, in turn, can become important allies to your future career development.

You can also gain a great deal by carefully studying those who are the best in your field: roll models with whom you may or may not have established a personal relationship. A former National Football League player with the New York Giants organization once told me a story about his teammates studying videotapes of retired players. His recollection involved an incident in the team locker room after a grueling preseason practice. He described how he observed several of his teammates huddled around a television screen. As he approached the group, he saw that they were watching old game tapes of Forrest Gregg, a member of the National Football League Hall of Fame. When he asked why they were watching a tape of a retired player who had not played in many years, one teammate responded simply, "Because he was the best."

Identify those who are the best in your profession. Outstanding career models are all around us. Take the time to identify those who have excelled and study them. Ask yourself what has contributed to their success. Ask them, too! Model their techniques, develop their habits, and use your creativity to integrate what you have learned into your own personal style to allow you to enhance your career development.

Career Management Tip #8
Knowledge and Skills: Start the Race Now

Again, I would be grossly remiss if I understated the importance of continuing developing your knowledge and skills. As I am sure, however, you have already surmised, this certainly is not the only ingredient to career success. I know of many, many individuals who are very bright, talented, and capable in their own right. But they have fallen short of developing their true career potential because they lack other critical ingredients to career success.

Approach your self-development as an ongoing, lifelong process. Be comfortable with who you are, but never feel there is not room to learn, grow, and improve upon your career success. You can always be better. This means investing in yourself to develop new skills, keeping current of trends and issues both within and outside your field, developing and operating technical skills and other competencies, refining your interpersonal skills, becoming a leader in your community and profession, and working hard to continuously expand your network of professional contacts and build new relationships.

Each day's workplace grows more competitive every day. Lewis Carroll perhaps said it best in *Alice In Wonderland:*

> *To stay where you are, you have to run as fast as you can. If you want to get ahead, you have to run twice as fast as that.*

Career Management Tip #9
Support: Who Can Help You?

Support can come from many sources: your boss, a mentor, your colleagues, your family and friends, your organization, prior employers, your staff, your secretary, and so on. Each of these sources of support have the potential to help vault your career development to new heights. We often take for granted or do not fully receive the support available to us. Sometimes we simply are not creative enough, or we are unwilling to examine how we can harness the valuable support resources available to us.

Most of us possess a wealth of potentially career-aiding resources much richer than we realize. In describing how he became a partner in a Fortune 500 home-building organization, one senior client pointed to the invaluable support his staff and organization offered. Without this support, he contended, he could not have realized the rapid progress in his career development he enjoyed. My client appreciated his boss for sending him to advanced management training programs at Ivy League schools, selecting him for high-visibility international assignments, and providing him with talented and ambitious staff members. He also appreciated his wife and two daughters who shared his vision for his career development. To his credit, he harnessed the sources of support available to him to accelerate his career development.

On the other hand, a lack of support, whether it be a spouse, staff member, or boss, can be devastating. The plight of many partners in a dual-career relationship during a corporate relocation of their transferred partner illustrates this well: these supportive partners have *chosen to* forsake their own career development for their partner's. After they have made the geographical relocation, however, they soon find themselves lacking the powerful support system offered by a network of professional contacts and former bosses who could potentially serve as referral sources and have knowledge of their new labor markets. Often, these relocated partners had attained levels of stature and success in their own careers comparable to what their transferred spouse had realized. After their relocation, they endure the lonely, emotional task of conducting a job campaign – a chore that is arduous enough for those fortunate to have an intact support system. Newly relocated partners find this career transition psychologically distressing. Their lot epitomizes the unfortunate fate of those lacking the many resources that a good support system can offer.

Take a thorough inventory of all the sources of support available to you. This includes not only your family and support that comes from work-related sources, but also support of professional contacts whom you may not have previously thought to access. One ambitious client was particularly adept at tapping into his colleagues' influence within the local business community. This client aspired to become part of a prestigious leadership program offered through the chamber of commerce in his city. His application had been denied the year before. The next year, he was determined more than ever not to be overlooked for this high-visibility opportunity that he knew could propel his career development. What did he do? He sought out a well-respected colleague who had held influential positions in the chamber and requested his help. His colleague was a friend he met through his Rotary club. The colleague gladly agreed to write a letter endorsing my client's application and send it to the chairperson of the selection committee. You can probably guess the outcome. The experience my client gained from completing the leadership program provided an invaluable opportunity for high-level exposure, developing a new network of executive level contacts, and recognition as an emerging business leader. Some label the client's tactic as tapping into the good-old-boy network; others call it smart careering.

Sometimes we try to accomplish more than is within our capability alone. Look around – there are likely several untapped sources of support that you can harness to help you attain your career objectives. Do not overlook the many resources available to you. Build a support base and actively seek out opportunities to reciprocate the goodwill others extend.

Career Management Tip #10
Career Skills: Learn How to Market Yourself

Talent alone will take you only so far in your career development. The real challenge is not getting people to recognize your skills and abilities, it is showing them how you can help them achieve their objectives. That means that you not only need to build relationships with those who have the power and influence to help promote your career aspirations, you also need to sell yourself as a potential vehicle that will help others achieve their aims. The lack of this critical ingredient is what too often separates those who break through barriers in their career development from those who plateau prematurely.

For better or worse, the business culture of the twenty-first century is one of close scrutiny of what will not quickly contribute to profit. Doing a good job and then waiting quietly in the wings for your due is a career development strategy that may have worked in another time. Today, however, it is like trying to find a record album at a music store. The approach is antiquated and, even if you find albums, you will likely find your selection very limited and you may end up listening to music that has little interest to you. A lack of confidence to oneself often accounts for why so many people are apprehensive about self-promotion.

True professionals gain attention without grandstanding. They seek out opportunities that endorse and validate their stature for them. How can you promote yourself with tact and good taste? Consider how you may be able to implement the following careering tactics.

- Identify key groups in which you wish to increase your exposure and stature. Research the issues of interest to these groups and develop opportunities to present your ideas. A well-planned circuit tour of industry and community groups, service clubs and professional organizations, and radio and television programs can go a long way in cultivating your image as an expert.

- Publish an article in your organization's newsletter, local business publication, or in a trade journal. Being "published" often adds to your credibility. Leaving behind reprints of your work at presentations you make can also be impressive.

- Volunteer to chair a committee or to undertake a high-visibility project within your organization, professional association, or community.

- Get to know the editor and writers of a local business publications in your community or within your profession. Develop a media list and update your contacts when you accomplish anything of significance. Once members of the media become familiar with you, they will be more apt to seek you out for a quote or possible story idea.

- Seek out key leadership positions. These opportunities could include important committees within your place of employment, boards of directors, officer-level positions in professional associations and community nonprofit organizations, or political appointments (mayoral, county, gubernatorial, or presidential).

- Consult with a public relations professional to plan how you can penetrate the audience you desire. This is a common practice for senior executives who move to a new area and are unfamiliar with how to access the power groups in their new community.

- Risk the potential rejection associated with nominating yourself or asking someone to nominate you for an award that will boost your stature within your profession.

All of the above tactics can give you positive exposure. Be patient but persistent in your careering activities. Also, beware of coming off too strongly in your self-presentation to the point where you may be at risk of intimidating your boss, colleagues, and other people of influence. Use an understated approach in which your accomplishments and implied endorsements gained through your careering activities speak for you.

Career Management Tip #11
Strike a Balance in Your Life:
Integrate Career and Personal Activities

Business executives today should be well aware of their need to strike a balance between their career and their personal life. The word "balance" is a common mantra we hear in many professional development programs. Yet, despite hearing this message repeatedly through the media and the corporate line, business people are actually working longer hours and growing more disgruntled about compromising the quality of lives on behalf of their employers. While the maxim, "Strike a Balance in Your Life " makes intuitive sense, it is obviously not an easy concept to implement. The smart career planner comes closest by integrating career and personal activities.

Psychologists cite some different life areas that contribute to a sense of well being and balance in humans: relationships, physical health, mental health, spirituality, community, leisure – and yes, work. The popular belief is that problems arise when a person becomes overextended in one or more of these areas and other vital areas, consequently, become impoverished.

The challenge of leading a balanced life while aggressively developing your career boils down to integrating these seven life areas. For instance, the astute career developer seeks leisure and community involvement activities that offer the opportunity for making and developing new business contacts. Whether it is the golf course, tennis courts, or your children's extracurricular activities, opportunities abound to mix business and pleasure. Use your creativity to plan how you can accomplish the dual objectives of leading a balanced life while simultaneously promoting your career development.

Career Management Tip #12
Create Luck: Be in the Right Places at the Right Times

The expression "creating luck" is not an oxymoron in career development. Lucky breaks do, of course, happen. You can enhance the chance of having a lucky break come your way by strategically placing yourself in situations where positive things are more likely to happen to you. One of my favorite examples involves a client who joined a private dining club, assumed a position on the club's board of directors, and struck up a friendship with another board of director's member, who happened to be the CEO of a large regional bank. As their relationship developed, my client was offered a key management position in his colleague's bank. Had he not accidently made the association with his future employer, he would have missed out on an outstanding career opportunity.

Lucky breaks sometime come from surprising places and circumstances. One salesperson, for instance, landed a key account by sitting next to a decision maker at a homeowner's association meeting. In another instance, an out-of-work accountant in a golf tournament was placed in a foursome in which he made a contact that led to a job interview and, ultimately, an offer. People who get lucky breaks have a knack for two things: (1) They seek out opportunities in which good things have a higher probability of happening to them, and (2) they are skilled at identifying and developing career advancement opportunities others overlook.

Opportunities are everywhere, but they are not likely to come to you without your effort. Clearly, a relationship exists between your ability to create luck and your ability to effectively network and market yourself. Keep your eyes open, but make sure you are looking in the right places.

Career Management Tip #13
Pride: Is It Driving You?

During my years of experience as a career counselor, I have met many accomplished individuals who, besides having established impressive records of career development and respect among their peers, have attained financial success. Certainly, these individuals could rest on their laurels and approach their career development in a more relaxed manner. Yet, I have found that most maintain the intensity and passion they had before they realized career success.

What continues to drive career overachievers? Invariably it is their pride. Pride is among the factors I have found to fuel an esteemed trial lawyer to continue litigating intense, challenging cases. I have seen pride at work in an affluent tutor who maintains a demanding schedule of teaching disadvantaged, learning-disabled children. Pride is also among the things that I believe drives many renowned university professors to continue delving into complex research studies and publishing well after they have earned the security of faculty tenure, and their continued efforts are unlikely to result in substantial financial gain.

Lack of pride in one's work and career development is usually evident and often disturbing. How do others sense whether you have pride in your work and career? When people go out of their way to perform well beyond the minimum expectations, pride is among the evident factors fueling extraordinary effort. Something is intrinsically rewarding about taking initiative or being personally sought to perform a task, feeling an overwhelming desire and sense of responsibility to perform it well and, at the end of the day, being viewed as one who can be trusted to do a thorough, competent job, attaining results few others could realize.

No matter what your work involves – manual labor or highly skilled tasks – I hope you are proud to do it. If not, that may be a strong signal that your work may not be well matched for you. Pride, work ethic, and career success are inextricably linked.

Obviously, those who display pride in their work are apt to be more frequently sought and offered career development opportunities than those who do not. What inferences do those important to your career development make about the pride you display in your work?

Career Management Tip #14
Power: Learn How to Use It

Much of my work during the past 20 years has involved consulting business organizations about individuals they are considering hiring or promoting. During these assessments I am particularly mindful of how those being considered for leadership positions would likely cultivate and use power to further the objectives that they and the organization hold.

Power, which refers to ability to influence others and resist their influence on us, is a concept some are weary to discuss or acknowledge. Perhaps this is because most of us have witnessed abuses of power and, thus, are apprehensive about prominently recognizing it for fear of being perceived as one who creates power or will not use it appropriately.

Understanding how power influences people and cultivating an effective power base will help you to attain your career objectives. Psychologists generally recognize six types of power:

- Reward power: Derived from the holder's ability to reward others.

- Coercive power: Derived from the holder's ability to punish others.

- Legitimate power: Derived from acknowledgment of the holder's valid authority in a given situation. Examples include power held by elected officials, police, and those with status in an organization because of their position on an organizational chart.

- Charismatic power: Derived from others' attraction to or desire to be like the holder of this source of power.

- Expert power: Derived from the belief that the power holder has special knowledge or expertise.

- Informational power: Derived from the holder's possession of a specific, desired piece of information.

Consider a situation, for example, in which your boss asks you to work overtime and you comply with this request. The type of power being exerted over you could be:

- coercive power, if you feel you must say yes to avoid being fired

- reward power, if you are offered overtime pay or bonuses

- legitimate power, if you recognize her or his valid authority

- expert power, if you trust that the boss knows more about the job, so that you yield to her or his having more facts than you about the necessity of having to work after regular work hours

- charismatic power, if the boss somehow inspires you and you desire to be more like your boss

- informational power, if you believe your boss possesses information about the future of the organization that would help you better plan your career development, and you wish to obtain this information

Commonly, one or more types of power can be operating at a given time, depending upon the situation. Further, different types of power can work in combination.

Those who combine expert and charismatic power tend to be most effective in gaining compliance and developing positive relationships. These sources of power are based more on the characteristics of the person than on position or the situation at hand, and a combination of their use is likely to result in greater acceptance of the leader and greater effectiveness, long term.

People who adeptly manage their career development recognize power as a reality in a work place, and learn to understand it and to wield it judiciously and appropriately. They also avoid coercive power, and do not over rely on legitimate or reward power. Remember – attaining your career objectives will likely require goodwill, support, and cooperation from others; inappropriate use of power will not facilitate these aims.

Summary

Nearly everyone at one time or another ponders the question of what lends to successful career development. Have you been doing a good job of managing your career? Careering activities, which are the activities beyond your actual work that promote your career development, are vital to accelerating the rate of your career development. These activities also allow you to control and manage your career more effectively. Consider specific actions and time frames for undertaking the following career management activities.

Career Management Activities

1. Key organizations or committees for me to join and become active in include:

2. To gain more visibility within my organization, business, community and profession, I will:

3. A person(s) with whom I will attempt to develop a mentor/protege relationship is(are):

4. To better market my career development, I will:

Chapter 7

∽

Conducting an Effective Job Search

Conducting an Effective Job Search

Chances are that you will undergo at least one job search during your career. Even if your immediate career decision does not involve conducting a job search, I would be remiss if I did not offer a few practical tips on conducting an effective, professional job search campaign. In a competitive labor market in which mergers, reorganizations, acquisitions, downsizings, and relocations are commonplace, developing job skills and knowing strategies that give you a competitive edge are beneficial.

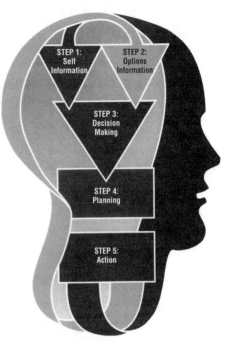

Most people agree that being able to secure a job in line with their career goals is one of the most important skills anyone can develop. We have all done it; however, few admit to being good at it. This chapter outlines several techniques that I have found effective. Figure 16 presents the methodology I advocate for those conducting a job search.

Preparing for the Labor Market

Too often, people looking for a job delve into the labor market before they are ready. They hurry to follow-up on want ads; get leads from friends, head hunters, and the like; and flood the Internet and post office with unsolicited resumes to organizations they know little about. When they do land a job interview and the prospective employer says, "Tell me, what type of job are you looking for," they too often give an answer they perceive the interviewer will welcome or they provide a vague, overrehearsed, or trite response like "more challenge," "growth potential," or "a chance to apply my skills."

Just as a good salesperson will carefully screen and qualify a prospective client before making a presentation, a well-prepared job seeker will absolutely not enter a job interview before answering two important questions. First, what is it that I want in my career, and how will the job I seek help me move closer to my ultimate career goal? And second, what organizations can provide experiences that will help me advance my aspired career path or objectives? These two questions are deceptively simple. Your preparation for the labor market should begin with a thorough understanding of yourself. Unless you have carefully inventoried your personal and work values, skills, interests, and personal circumstances that could impact various career decisions, you are not ready to solicit job interviews, and you are very likely doing yourself a disservice.

Consulting a professional career counselor and completing the activities recommended earlier in Decision Time will help you to reinforce the career direction you choose. There are shortcuts to this assessment, although they inevitably lead to trial-and-error career development. Only after you can clearly state your career objective (as I have been suggesting throughout this book, this is much simpler than it sounds) should you proceed with your job search. The next steps involve creating a resume that reflects your objective in targeting organizations that promise to be a good match for your goals.

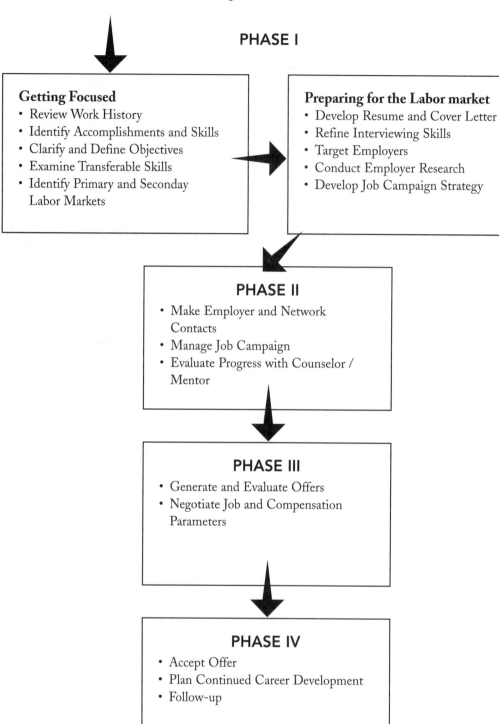

Figure 16. Recommended approach to coordinating a job search

Some quick tips on developing your resume:

- *Stress your accomplishments.* Anyone can pat themselves on the back and trumpet self-serving accolades such as "effective leader" or "results-oriented executive," but, what does this really mean? Identify accomplishments that speak for you and subtly portray that you are a savvy professional adept at capitalizing on opportunities and solving problems. For instance, emphasize accomplishments such as new business generated, dollars saved, customer complaints reduced, budgetary responsibilities, and supervisory scope.

- *Be sure to feature your value-added qualities.* That is, highlight the experiences, skills, and knowledge you possess that separate you from the pack of other candidates competing against you.

- *Select a format that is visually inviting and easy to scan.* Most hiring authorities spend 60 seconds or less reviewing resumes during initial screenings. Using headings effectively, featuring key information by underlining or using different type faces, and logically organizing information will help optimize the time decision makers commit to their first review of your resume. People do judge a book by its cover. Make sure your book cover – your resume – serves you well. Use good paper stock and avoid dark colors.

- *Remember, the purpose of your resume is to whet prospective employers' interest in your background, not to retrace all the details of your career development.* Preferably, keep your resume to one page, and definitely not more than two pages. Pictures are almost always inappropriate on a resume (exceptions include applications for job such as modeling assignments and some security positions). Also, avoid cute language and "cookie cutter" phrases that are all too common in most resumes.

- *Modify your resume from time to time.* Experiment with new formats, changes to phrasing, and how you feature your skills and accomplishments. Get feedback from colleagues and, if possible, from human resources professionals. Ideally, each resume and cover letter you submit should address and be tailored to the position in question.

You can research prospective employers, for example, by consulting industry directories, using information available through the Chamber of Commerce and other community organizations, talking to people who are employed at organizations that interest you, visiting Web sites, and reviewing annual reports or other literature your prospective employers publish. Go beyond gathering basic personnel-related information; learn about the organization's strategic plans, new markets it may be planning to enter, industry trends, and its competition. Your research will enhance your confidence and preparation before meeting prospective employers. If you meet with potential employers, your preparation may lead to opportunities to meet with other viable employers later.

Succeeding in the Labor Market

A positive, can-do attitude is essential to succeeding in the labor market. Anything less will almost certainly compromise your career development.

Searching for employment can be humbling and disappointing. Hopes are sometimes dashed, and long periods of waiting are common. Internalizing the negative experiences that arise from a job search is self-defeating, and I encourage you to be quick to dispel symptoms of this sort. Prolonged job searches all too often spiral into a nonproductive, self-fulfilling prophecy in which job seekers begin questioning their value in the workplace.

The importance of perspective and a positive attitude about seeking employment was punctuated in a presentation I observed several years ago while consulting with an international employment agency. A trainer, with two flip charts flanking her, began by eliciting from her audience composed of employment placement specialists their views on who, historically, have been perceived as the lowest members of society. A few snickers emerge from the audience as they offered occupations such as lawyer and tax collector. The conversation grew more serious, and ultimately ended with the group's agreement that beggars and those in search of handouts have, historically, been perceived as the lowest members of society. All of the responses were recorded on one flip chart.

Next, the trainer asked her audience to consider the converse: that is, historically, which members of society have been perceived as most valued. This discussion generated more energy, and the group began by identifying hunters and those who provide for others. Examples of contemporary occupations such as successful salespeople, soon followed. Again, all of this information was recorded on the second flip chart.

With the two contrasting sets of information on the flip charts, the trainer provided a pithy analogy to job searching: too many people approach their job searches as "job beggars" rather than "job hunters." That is, they subliminally communicate to prospective employers a "please hire me" message rather than selectively hunting for and confidently pursuing desired jobs. If you were an employer, would you rather hire a "job beggar" or a "job hunter?" Again, beware of "job beggar" symptoms that may creep up as you pursue your job campaign.

Your job search likely will include activities such as generating leads, interviewing, writing follow-up letter and making up follow-up calls, touring prospective workplaces and, in some cases, taking tests, being evaluated in an assessment center, and making presentations to prospective employers. Managing an effective job campaign requires discipline, perseverance, and sound strategy.

I have found that those who secure the jobs they want more often than not approach their job campaign in an organized, systematic manner. To facilitate your efforts I have included several organizational forms in Appendix F. The appendix includes a weekly job search plan to help you manage your overall job campaign strategy; a form for planning your daily efforts is also included. Other forms in the appendix will help you stay focused and obtain important information for future reference during job interviews. The final form will help you scrutinize your job offers. I recommend that you make photocopies of the forms in Appendix F and use them diligently throughout your job search campaign.

Maintaining an ongoing, consistent, high level of effort in your job search is critical; I cannot overemphasize this. Too often job searchers diminish their efforts when they believe themselves close to securing a job offer. Unfortunately, the offer that appears close to consummation is sometimes suspended, rescinded, or extended to another individual. This leaves the job searcher deflated psychologically, and contributes to a loss of momentum and valuable time in the overall job search process.

Also, be cautious about assuming that a great deal of activity is necessarily going to generate interest from prospective employers. Sending out dozens of resumes by e-mail, for example, is something that can be done quickly and with little effort. While the number of these contacts can be impressive, your efforts will probably not generate a proportionate amount of consideration of you as a job candidate. In fact, when solicited, mass mailings of resumes and job applications – whether by regular mail, fax, or e-mail – notoriously generates extremely low interest. My caution is not to avoid using this medium; rather, avoid being lulled into a false sense of confidence that can arise when one has initiated a great deal of activity.

Job interviews are one of the most important parts of your job campaign. The difference between candidates who realize success in generating job offers and those who do not does not always relate to qualifications for the position in question. Quite often, a candidate with superior job-finding skills prevails. Like any product or service available, packaging and image often separate products high in demand from those that get less attention. Candidates who secure attractive job offers quickly not only appear qualified in terms of their ability to perform the job, they effectively project attributions of confidence, teamwork, and knowledge about the organization and how their skills can contribute to its success.

When preparing for your job interviews, remember that those who will evaluate you are usually not professional interviewers. Most interviewers lack training and experience in assessing job candidates; the average hiring authority makes less than three selection decisions per year, and often perceives the interviewing process as a necessary evil that goes along with her or his other job responsibilities. Therefore, I recommend you consider how you can facilitate your perspective employer's efforts to discover and understand how you can help the organization solve current and projected problems.

Viewing a debate among top political candidates provides insight into how true professionals can defuse no-win, sensitive questions and manage to end on a positive note by recapping major successes and accomplishments to present themselves in a positive light.

Successful job candidates adopt a similar strategy; they plan before the interview to feature three or four of their strongest attributes into their interview question responses, rather than leaving their faith in the hands of a novice interviewer who may not pose a question that enables the important information to emerge. And, of course, strong job interviewers anticipate and plan answers to problem questions – such as "What were you doing during the 6-month gap on your resume?" or "How do you explain your job change from a manager to a staff employee?" – before they are asked, and so should you!

Finally, remember that your job campaign does not end until you have accepted an offer. Too often people lessen their job search intensity when they perceive an attractive offer is impending. If, for whatever reason, the job is not offered to them, the job candidate often experiences a psychological setback and loses valuable momentum and time. Persistence and thoughtful restrategizing mark successful seekers. Keep at your job search until you feel confident that an offer extended to you represents the best you can realistically secure, and that the job can provide an opportunity for you to move ahead in your career plans. Keep your self-assessment summary form from *Decision Time* handy, and refer to it as you evaluate your job offers.

The Final Analysis: Long- and Short-Term Considerations

Ideally, your efforts will generate more than a single job offer. How well you negotiate your offers can have important implications for both your short-term and long-term career development that can go far beyond your salary. A skilled negotiator, for instance, may negotiate a title and compensation package at the time the actual hire is made that could otherwise have taken several years to attain.

Your negotiating power is always greatest during the brief period after you have received an offer and before you have formally accepted the decision and actually begin working. Once you have assumed your new job, it is nearly impossible to go back to your boss and ask for something more than what you have already agreed to accept.

Every negotiation you engage should involve three steps:

1. *Determine the negotiables – look beyond your salary.* For instance, negotiables may include title, performance review dates, discretionary time to pursue other interests, allowances for attending conventions and other professional development activities, and support resources to help you perform your job. Only the boundaries of your creativity limit the negotiables that you identify.

2. *Identify your negotiating range – determine beforehand the least you are willing to accept in a compensation package and the most you can possibly justify.* This will require wage research, and your ability to carefully identify and articulate your value-added features as a prospective employee. Of course, you will keep your negotiating range concealed as this phase of the hiring process progresses. If you become involved in a complicated negotiation with details such as an employment agreement, relocation, profit sharing, and severance pay, consider consulting both an attorney and a career counselor. Also, request your job offer and associated details in writing; this can be helpful if future disputes arise.

3. *Determine a negotiating strategy – begin the negotiation by suggesting a compensation package at the top of your negotiation range, or maximum supportable position.* The "one trip to the well" adage definitely applies to negotiating a job offer. Why not start by asking for the most you can reasonably justify? Also, plan ahead those negotiables that you are willing to concede, if necessary. Negotiating is truly an art that you can learn and refine through self-study, coaching, and practice. Without sound negotiation skills, you risk losing valuable time and opportunities to attain your long-term career goals.

Before accepting a job offer, reflect back on the information you learned about yourself when you began your job campaign. That is, does this job promise to be a good fit between your work values, interests, skills, personal circumstances, and long-term aspirations?

Summary

Many people greet the end of their job campaigns with a sign of relief: the interviewing, anxiety, rejection letters, waiting, and concerns over finances are, at least for the moment, over. Keep in mind, however, the dynamic nature of career development. Career development is not a discrete, point-in-time activity; it is a process that we undergo throughout our lives.

The job you land is, of course, vital to your long-term career plan. True professionals develop plans that consider questions like: How will this job contribute to my short-term and long-term career goals? Is this job a positive step toward my long-term career goals, or is it merely a short-term, convenient solution? Those who develop successful, fulfilling careers are always mindful of these questions – even when not searching for a job.

Chapter 8

❧

Moving On

Moving On

Alas! how swift moments fly!
How flash the years along!
Scarce here, yet gone already by,
The burden of a song.
See childhood, youth, and manhood pass.
And age with furrowed brow!
Time was – Time shall be – drain the glass –
But where in time is now?

*– **John Quincy Adams**, The Hour Glass*

Our sixth President's poem reminds us that time and career development are tightly woven. If you feel unfulfilled, have a lack of focus, or believe you are in a dead-end career path, you have no time to waste in changing your course. Unfortunately, fear of change, lack of self-confidence, and procrastination are the culprits that often prevent well-laid plans from fruition.

Once you have committed to your career decision and drafted a viable career plan, waste no time. Get on with your plan, without charging ahead recklessly, oblivious to the need for fine-tuning. You can be sure that at least some, and possibly considerable, modifications will be needed as you progress. By failing to get started, however, you are wasting valuable time and conceding your career development to chance. Begin cautiously, but do begin!

After you have completed your work with Decision Time, keep it nearby. Use it to monitor your progress and to help you make future career decisions. Also, be sure to adopt a mentor – someone who has surmounted the challenges that you have yet to encounter on your way to your aspired career objective. A good mentor provides invaluable guidance and support that can make a critical difference to your success.

Pursuing your career objective may take you down any number of paths: advanced training, entering or reentering the workforce, changing occupations, advancing to a more responsible position within your current place of employment or elsewhere, starting your own business, preparing for retirement, and so on. Whichever path you take, like most people, you will probably experience some moments of self-doubt and insecurity about your decision. Most people do. People who attain satisfying careers, however, do not feebly abandon their career objectives when setbacks occur. They reexamine their career plans, make necessary adjustments, and persist – mindful of the promise their objective holds: the chance to become more self-fulfilled. Settling for anything less is to compromise life satisfaction.

Appendix A

Interest Activity Cards

These cards are designed to help you better understand
your career interests.

VERY INTERESTING

INTERESTING

SOMEWHAT INTERESTING

UNINTERESTING

Department Store Manager
Directs and coordinates, through subordinate managerial personnel, activities of department store selling lines of merchandise.

Travel Guide
Arranges transportation and other accommodations for groups of tourists, following planned itinerary and escorts groups during entire trip.

Director of Welfare Agency
Directs agency or major function of public or voluntary organization providing services in social welfare field to individuals, groups, or community.

Medical Laboratory Technician
Performs routine tests in medical laboratory to provide data for use in diagnosis and treatment of disease.

Payroll Clerk
Compiles payroll data, and enters data or computes and post wages, and reconciles errors, to maintain payroll records using computer or calculator.

Marriage Counselor
Provides individual, marital, and family counseling services to adults and children, to assist clients to identify personal and interactive problems and to achieve effective adjustment.

Salesperson
Sells merchandise to individuals in store or showroom, utilizing knowledge of products sold.

Probation Officer
Counsels juvenile or adult offenders in activities related to legal conditions of probation or parole.

Novelist
Writes original prose material for publication. Conducts research, organizes material, develops theme, order, and story line. Reviews, revises, and corrects material to submit for publication.

Court Reporter
Records examination, testimony, judicial opinions, and other proceedings by machine shorthand or recording device. Uses typewriter or computer to transcribe material.

Locomotive Engineer
Drives electric, diesel-electric, or gas-turbine-electric locomotive, interpreting train orders, train signals, and railroad rules and regulations, to transport passengers or freight.

Researcher
Analyzes verbal or statistical data to prepare reports and studies for use by professional workers in a variety of areas, such as science, social science, law, medicine, or politics.

Independent Research Scientist
Conducts experiments or investigations, utilizing knowledge of scientific disciplines, to develop understanding of such topics as materials, soils, animals, crops, food, and the environment.

Radio Operator
Operates and keeps in repair radiotelephone transmitter and receiving equipment for commercial communication.

Machinist
Sets up and operates machines and machining centers to fabricate metallic and nonmetallic parts, and fits and assembles machined parts into complete units.

Freelance Writer
Prepares assigned or unassigned articles from knowledge of topic, supplemented by additional study and research. Submits and discusses copy with editor for approval.

Bank Teller
Receives and pays out money, and keeps records of money and negotiable instruments involved in financial transactions.

Business Executive
Directs and coordinates activities of business organization to obtain optimum efficiency and economy of operations and maximize profits.

Estimator
Analyzes blueprints, specifications, proposals, and other documentation to prepare time, cost and labor estimates for products, projects, or services, applying knowledge of specialized techniques and principles.

Surveyor
Plans and directs work of survey parties engaged in surveying earthís surface to determine precise location and measurements of elevations, areas, and contours for construction, mapmaking, and land division, titles, or other purposes.

Tax Expert
Audits financial records to determine tax liability and to advise.

Personal Counselor
Counsels individuals and provides assistance in understanding and overcoming social and emotional problems. May provide group educational and vocational guidance services.

Biologist
Studies basic principles of plant and animal life, such as origin, relationship, development, anatomy, and functions.

Speech Therapist
Specializes in diagnosis and treatment of speech and language problems, and engages in scientific study of human communication.

Bookkeeper
Keeps records of financial transactions for establishment, using calculator and computer.

Elected Public Official
Assists in direction and coordination of the administration of government in accordance with policies determined by city council or other authorized elected officials.

Botanist
Studies development and life processes, physiology, heredity, environment, distribution, anatomy, and economic value of plants for application in such fields as agronomy, forestry, horticulture, and pharmacology.

Credit Investigator
Investigates persons or business establishments applying for credit, employment, insurance, loans, or settlement of claims.

Advertising Executive
Plans and executes advertising policies of organization.

Playwright
Writes original plays, such as tragedies, comedies, or dramas, or adapts themes from fictional, historical, or narrative sources, for dramatic presentation.

Technical Writer
Prepares and writes technical, scientific, medical, or other material for publication with or independent from manufacturing, research, and related activities.

Physicist
Conducts research into phases of physical phenomena, develops theories and laws on basis of observation and experiments, and devises methods to apply laws and theories of physics to industry, medicine, and other fields.

Appendix A: Interest Activity Cards

Editor of Scientific Journal
Directs and coordinates activities of writers engaged in preparing technical, scientific, medical, or other material for publication with or independent from manufacturing, research, and related activities.

Clinical Psychologist
Diagnoses or evaluates mental and emotional disorders of individuals, and administers programs of treatment.

Social Worker
Counsels and aids individuals and families requiring assistance.

Firefighter
Controls and extinguishes fires, protects life and property, and maintains equipment as volunteer or employee of city, township, or industrial plant.

Social Science Teacher
Teaches social science subjects to students in public or private secondary schools.

Manufacturer's Representative
Sells single, allied, diversified, or multiline products to wholesalers or other customers for one or more manufacturers on commission basis.

Musical Arranger
Transcribes musical composition for orchestra, band, choral group, or individual to adapt composition to particular style for which it was not originally written.

Electrician
Plans layout, installs, and repairs wiring, electrical fixtures, apparatus, and control equipment.

Life Insurance Salesperson
Explains, recommends and sells insurance to new and current clients.

Symphony Conductor
Conducts instrumental music groups, such as orchestras and dance bands.

Financial Analyst
Analyzes financial information to forecast business, industry, and economic conditions, for use in making investment decisions.

Musician
Plays musical instrument as soloist or as member of musical group, such as orchestra or band, to entertain audience.

Tree Surgeon
Prunes and treats ornamental and shade trees and shrubs in yards and parks to improve their appearance, health, and value.

Fish and Wildlife Specialist
Patrols assigned area to prevent game law violations, investigates reports of damage to crops and property by wildlife, and compiles biological data.

Restaurant Manager
Coordinates food service activities of hotel, restaurant, or other similar establishment or at social functions.

Dispatcher
Operates communication equipment to receive incoming calls for assistance and dispatches personnel.

Appendix A: Interest Activity Cards

Comptroller
Directs financial activities of organization or subdivision of organization.

Physical Therapist
Plans and administers medically prescribed physical therapy treatment to patients suffering from injuries, or muscle, nerve, joint, and bone diseases, to restore function, relieve pain, and prevent disability.

Geologist
Studies composition, structure, and history of earth's crust.

Zoologist
Studies origin, interrelationships, classification, life histories, habits, life processes, diseases, relation to environment, growth and development, genetics, and distribution of animals.

Budget Analyst
Analyzes current and past budgets, prepares and justifies budget requests, and allocates funds according to spending priorities.

Youth Camp Director
Administers and implements youth — serving organization's program and services.

Bus Driver
Drives bus to transport passengers over specified routes to local or distant points according to time schedule.

Sculptor
Designs and constructs three-dimensional art works, utilizing any combination of mediums, methods, and techniques.

Entertainer
Entertains audience by exhibiting special skills.
Radio/TV Announcer
Announces radio and television programs to audience.

Certified Public Accountant
Applies principles of accounting to analyze financial information and prepare financial reports.

Journalist
Selects subject matter based on personal interest or receives specific assignment from publisher and writes material for publication.

Real Estate Sales Agent
Rents, buys, and sells property for clients on commission basis.

Actor
Portrays role in dramatic production to interpret character or present characterization to audience.

Meteorologist
Analyzes and interprets meteorological data gathered by surface and upper-air stations, satellites, and radar to prepare reports and forecasts for public and other users.

Investment Manager
Sells financial products and services to clients for investment purposes, applying knowledge of securities, investment plans, market conditions, regulations, and financial situation of clients.

Anthropologist
Makes comparative studies in relation to distribution, origin, evolution, and races of humans, cultures they have created, and their distribution and physical characteristics.

Business Teacher
Instructs students in commercial subjects, such as typing, filing, secretarial procedures, business mathematics, office equipment use, and personality development, in business schools or training programs.

Airplane Mechanic
Services, repairs, and overhauls aircraft and aircraft engines to ensure airworthiness.

Artist
Draws or paints variety of original subject material, such as landscapes, portraits, still lives, and abstracts, using watercolors, oils, pen and ink, charcoal, pencil, acrylics, or other mediums.

Astronomer
Observes and interprets celestial phenomena and relates research to basic scientific knowledge or to practical problems, such as navigation.

School Principal
Directs and coordinates educational, administrative, and counseling activities of primary or secondary school.

Computer Repair Technician
Repairs computers following blueprints and manufacturer's specifications, using hand tools and test instruments.

Buyer
Purchases merchandise or commodities for resale.

Auto Mechanic
Repairs and overhauls automobiles, buses, trucks, and other automotive vehicles.

Carpenter
Constructs, erects, installs, and repairs structures and fixtures of wood, plywood, and wallboard, using carpenter's hand tools and power tools and conforming to local building codes.

Truck Driver
Drives truck to transport materials to and from specified destinations.

Cartoonist
Draws cartoons for publications to amuse readers and interpret or illustrate news highlights, advertising, stories, or articles.

School Counselor
Aids students with behavioral, mental, emotional, vocational, or physical problems.

Construction Inspector
Inspects and oversees construction of bridges, buildings, dams, highways, and other types of construction work to ensure that procedures and materials comply with plans and specification.

Sales Manager
Directs staffing, training, and performance evaluations to develop and control sales program.

High School Teacher
Teaches one or more subjects to students in public or private secondary schools.

Composer
Writes musical compositions.

Bank Examiner
Examines and analyzes accounting records to determine financial status of establishment and prepares financial reports concerning operating procedures.

Chemist
Conducts research, analysis, and experimentation on substances, for such purposes as product and process development and application, quantitative and qualitative analysis, and improvement of analytical methodologies.

Military Officer
Advises and assists commander on such matters as troop welfare, health, and morale.

Mechanical Engineer
Researches, develops, plans, and designs mechanical and electromechanical products and systems.

Computer Programmer
Writes, tests, and maintains computer programs which provide instructions computers must follow to perform their function.

Lawyer
Conducts criminal and civil lawsuits, draws up legal documents, advises clients as to legal rights, and practices other phases of law.

Appendix B

o*net™ Career Exploration Tools

O*NET™ Occupations Combined List:

Interests and Work Values, v. 3.0

(For use with your Interest Profiler and Work Importance Locator instruments' results)

Table of Contents

Table of Contents (continued)

To help you explore careers, occupations have been listed by Job Zone for each Interest/Work Value category. The majority of occupations were included in the groups based on their highest interest and highest work value. Occupations with * beside the occupational title were included in the groups based on their highest interest and second highest work value. Occupations with ** beside the occupational title were included in the groups based on their highest interest and third highest work value. Occupations with *** beside the occupational title were included in the groups based on their second highest interest and highest work value. Data are not currently available for 74 O*NET-SOC occupations. These occupations do not appear in this list.

Special Notice: Proper Use of Interest Profiler/Work Importance Locator Results

Interest Profiler *and* **Work Importance Locator** *results* **should be used** *for career exploration and vocational counseling purposes only. Results are designed to assist clients in identifying their interests and work values and using them to identify occupations that may satisfy their interests and what is most important to them in an occupation.*

Interest Profiler *and* **Work Importance Locator** *results* **should not be used** *for employment or hiring decisions. Employers, educational programs or other job related programs should not use* **Interest Profiler** *or* **Work Importance Locator** *results for applicant screening for jobs or training programs. The relationship between results on the* **Interest Profiler** *and* **Work Importance Locator** *and success in particular jobs or training programs has not been determined.*

Interests and Work Values Worksheet

On the following pages are the occupations that are linked with the Interest Areas and the Work Values. They are listed in Interest Area/Work Value combinations. Occupations are grouped by Job Zone under each Interest/Work Value heading.

Below, please **circle** your Primary and Secondary Interests from the Interest Profiler:

Primary Interest:

R I A S E C

Secondary Interest:

R I A S E C

Also, **write** your two highest Work Values from the Work Importance Locator in the spaces below:

Achievement   **Independence**   **Recognition**   **Relationships**   **Support**   **Working Conditions**

Highest Work Value _____   **Next Highest Work Value** _____

Please **circle** your Job Zone(s) below:

Current Job Zone: 1 2 3 4 5   **Future Job Zone: 1 2 3 4 5**

To look at occupations linked with your Primary Interest Area and your highest Work Value, find the tab for your Primary Interest Area. Look within that section for the heading that includes your highest Work Value. The occupations are listed there by Job Zone. *For example, if your Primary Interest Area is Social and your highest Work Value is Working Conditions, you would pick the tab for Social and look for the heading Social—Working Conditions. If your Job Zone is Job Zone 2, you would look for the occupations grouped under Job Zone 2—Social—Working Conditions.*

Follow the same procedure to look at occupations linked with your Secondary Interest Areas and your next highest Work Value.

Write below the O∗NET occupations you have picked to explore:

O∗NET-SOC#	O∗NET-SOC Title
1. _____	_____
2. _____	_____
3. _____	_____
4. _____	_____
5. _____	_____
6. _____	_____
7. _____	_____
8. _____	_____
9. _____	_____
10. _____	_____

REALISTIC

REALISTIC — ACHIEVEMENT

JOB ZONE 1 — REALISTIC — ACHIEVEMENT

O*NET-SOC#	O*NET-SOC Title	O*NET-SOC#	O*NET-SOC Title
45-4011.00	Forest and Conservation Workers	51-9061.05	Production Inspectors, Testers, Graders, Sorters,
51-9123.00	Painting, Coating, and Decorating Workers*		Samplers, Weighers**
51-5023.09	Printing Press Machine Operators and Tenders*	51-9141.00	Semiconductor Processors**

(To find more occupations, look at other job zones in this combination or refer to the Interest and Work Value Master Lists.)

JOB ZONE 2 — REALISTIC — ACHIEVEMENT

O*NET-SOC#	O*NET-SOC Title	O*NET-SOC#	O*NET-SOC Title
45-2091.00	Agricultural Equipment Operators	29-2012.00	Medical and Clinical Laboratory Technicians
49-3023.02	Automotive Specialty Technicians	51-9082.00	Medical Appliance Technicians
47-2031.03	Carpenter Assemblers and Repairers	49-3052.00	Motorcycle Mechanics
49-9092.00	Commercial Divers	33-2011.01	Municipal Fire Fighters
29-2041.00	Emergency Medical Technicians and Paramedics***	41-4011.01	Sales Representatives, Agricultural***
51-6092.00	Fabric and Apparel Patternmakers	41-4011.03	Sales Representatives, Electrical/Electronic***
33-2021.01	Fire Inspectors***	41-4011.04	Sales Representatives, Mechanical Equipment and
27-1023.00	Floral Designers***		Supplies***
33-2011.02	Forest Fire Fighters	51-6041.00	Shoe and Leather Workers and Repairers
33-2022.00	Forest Fire Inspectors and Prevention Specialists	47-2044.00	Tile and Marble Setters
51-9071.06	Gem and Diamond Workers	51-2093.00	Timing Device Assemblers, Adjusters, and
39-5091.00	Makeup Artists, Theatrical and Performance***		Calibrators

JOB ZONE 3 — REALISTIC — ACHIEVEMENT

O*NET-SOC#	O*NET-SOC Title	O*NET-SOC#	O*NET-SOC Title
49-3011.03	Aircraft Body and Bonded Structure Repairers	49-3041.00	Farm Equipment Mechanics
49-3021.00	Automotive Body and Related Repairers	33-3051.02	Highway Patrol Pilots
49-3023.01	Automotive Master Mechanics	49-3051.00	Motorboat Mechanics
47-2021.00	Brickmasons and Blockmasons	49-3053.00	Outdoor Power Equipment and Other Small
49-3031.00	Bus and Truck Mechanics and Diesel Engine		Engine Mechanics
	Specialists	51-9194.01	Precision Etchers and Engravers, Hand or Machine
51-7011.00	Cabinetmakers and Bench Carpenters	27-4013.00	Radio Operators
19-4031.00	Chemical Technicians	49-3043.00	Rail Car Repairers
17-3011.02	Civil Drafters	47-2031.02	Rough Carpenters
49-2094.00	Electrical and Electronics Repairers, Commercial	51-9071.02	Silversmiths
	and Industrial Equipment	27-4014.00	Sound Engineering Technicians
47-2111.00	Electricians	51-9195.03	Stone Cutters and Carvers
17-3012.01	Electronic Drafters	49-9063.02	Stringed Instrument Repairers and Tuners
51-9194.02	Engravers/Carvers		

---

* Occupation included based on its highest interest area and second highest work value.
** Occupation included based on its highest interest area and third highest work value.
*** Occupation included based on its second highest interest area and highest work value.

REALISTIC — ACHIEVEMENT (continued)

JOB ZONE 4 — REALISTIC — ACHIEVEMENT

O*NET-SOC#	O*NET-SOC Title	O*NET-SOC#	O*NET-SOC Title
49-3011.02	Aircraft Engine Specialists	17-3013.00	Mechanical Drafters
49-3011.01	Airframe-and-Power-Plant Mechanics	17-3027.00	Mechanical Engineering Technicians
53-2011.00	Airline Pilots, Copilots, and Flight Engineers	49-3042.00	Mobile Heavy Equipment Mechanics, Except Engines
17-3011.01	Architectural Drafters	51-4061.00	Model Makers, Metal and Plastic
47-2031.05	Boat Builders and Shipwrights	51-7031.00	Model Makers, Wood
27-4012.00	Broadcast Technicians	33-1021.01	Municipal Fire Fighting and Prevention Supervisors
17-3022.00	Civil Engineering Technicians	51-7032.00	Patternmakers, Wood
17-2051.00	Civil Engineers	51-9071.05	Pewter Casters and Finishers
53-2012.00	Commercial Pilots	51-5022.03	Photoengravers
47-2031.01	Construction Carpenters	47-2152.01	Pipe Fitters
17-3023.03	Electrical Engineering Technicians	29-2034.01	Radiologic Technologists
17-3023.01	Electronics Engineering Technicians	47-2022.00	Stonemasons
51-9195.04	Glass Blowers, Molders, Benders, and Finishers		
51-9071.01	Jewelers		

JOB ZONE 5 — REALISTIC — ACHIEVEMENT

O*NET-SOC#	O*NET-SOC Title	O*NET-SOC#	O*NET-SOC Title
17-2011.00	Aerospace Engineers***	17-2161.00	Nuclear Engineers***
29-1061.00	Anesthesiologists***	29-1022.00	Oral and Maxillofacial Surgeons***
29-9091.00	Athletic Trainers***	29-1023.00	Orthodontists***
19-1020.01	Biologists***	17-2171.00	Petroleum Engineers
17-2041.00	Chemical Engineers***	19-2012.00	Physicists***
29-1011.00	Chiropractors***	17-2111.03	Product Safety Engineers***
29-1021.00	Dentists, General***	29-1024.00	Prosthodontists***
25-1032.00	Engineering Teachers, Postsecondary***	41-9031.00	Sales Engineers***
19-2041.00	Environmental Scientists and Specialists, Including Health***	27-1013.04	Sculptors***
		27-1027.01	Set Designers***
19-2042.01	Geologists***	53-5031.00	Ship Engineers
17-1012.00	Landscape Architects***	29-1067.00	Surgeons***
17-2121.02	Marine Architects	29-1131.00	Veterinarians***
17-2121.01	Marine Engineers	19-1023.00	Zoologists and Wildlife Biologists***

* Occupation included based on its highest interest area and second highest work value.
** Occupation included based on its highest interest area and third highest work value.
*** Occupation included based on its second highest interest area and highest work value.

REALISTIC — INDEPENDENCE

JOB ZONE 1 — REALISTIC — INDEPENDENCE

(No occupations for this combination in this job zone. To find occupations, look at other job zones in this combination or refer to the Interest and Work Value Master Lists.)

JOB ZONE 2 — REALISTIC — INDEPENDENCE

O*NET-SOC#	O*NET-SOC Title	O*NET-SOC#	O*NET-SOC Title
49-3091.00	Bicycle Repairers*	45-3021.00	Hunters and Trappers
33-2022.00	Forest Fire Inspectors and Prevention Specialists*	53-5022.00	Motorboat Operators
51-7021.00	Furniture Finishers*	53-6051.04	Railroad Inspectors**

JOB ZONE 3 — REALISTIC — INDEPENDENCE

O*NET-SOC#	O*NET-SOC Title	O*NET-SOC#	O*NET-SOC Title
45-2021.00	Animal Breeders	47-1011.02	First-Line Supervisors and Manager/Supervisors-Extractive Workers***
39-2011.00	Animal Trainers***		
47-4011.00	Construction and Building Inspectors***	35-1012.00	First-Line Supervisors/Managers of Food Preparation and Serving Workers***
51-9194.03	Etchers		
11-9012.00	Farmers and Ranchers	51-1011.00	First-Line Supervisors/Managers of Production and Operating Workers***
45-1011.01	First-Line Supervisors and Manager/Supervisors - Agricultural Crop Workers***		
45-1011.03	First-Line Supervisors and Manager/Supervisors - Animal Care Workers, Except Livestock	53-1031.00	First-Line Supervisors/Managers of Transportation and Material-Moving Machine and Vehicle Operators***
45-1011.02	First-Line Supervisors and Manager/Supervisors - Animal Husbandry Workers***	33-3031.00	Fish and Game Wardens
		39-9031.00	Fitness Trainers and Aerobics Instructors***
45-1011.06	First-Line Supervisors and Manager/Supervisors - Fishery Workers	37-1011.02	Janitorial Supervisors***
		51-5022.07	Platemakers
45-1011.04	First-Line Supervisors and Manager/Supervisors - Horticultural Workers	41-4011.06	Sales Representatives, Instruments***
		51-9071.02	Silversmiths
37-1012.02	First-Line Supervisors and Manager/Supervisors - Landscaping Workers	51-6093.00	Upholsterers

---

* Occupation included based on its highest interest area and second highest work value.
** Occupation included based on its highest interest area and third highest work value.
*** Occupation included based on its second highest interest area and highest work value.

REALISTIC — INDEPENDENCE (continued)

JOB ZONE 4 — REALISTIC — INDEPENDENCE

O*NET-SOC#	O*NET-SOC Title	O*NET-SOC#	O*NET-SOC Title
11-9011.02	Agricultural Crop Farm Managers***	19-1012.00	Food Scientists and Technologists***
19-3091.02	Archeologists***	19-1032.00	Foresters
51-5022.04	Camera Operators	19-3092.00	Geographers***
35-1011.00	Chefs and Head Cooks***	37-1012.01	Lawn Service Managers***
15-1071.01	Computer Security Specialists***	19-2032.00	Materials Scientists***
11-9021.00	Construction Managers***	17-2141.00	Mechanical Engineers
39-3092.00	Costume Attendants***	17-2151.00	Mining and Geological Engineers, Including Mining Safety Engineers***
51-6052.02	Custom Tailors		
45-1011.05	First-Line Supervisors and Manager/Supervisors - Logging Workers	11-9011.01	Nursery and Greenhouse Managers***
		19-1031.03	Park Naturalists***
47-1011.01	First-Line Supervisors and Manager/Supervisors- Construction Trades Workers***	51-9195.05	Potters
		53-5021.01	Ship and Boat Captains***
49-1011.00	First-Line Supervisors/Managers of Mechanics, Installers, and Repairers***	19-1031.01	Soil Conservationists***
		51-5022.06	Strippers
11-9011.03	Fish Hatchery Managers***	27-2012.05	Technical Directors/Managers

JOB ZONE 5 — REALISTIC — INDEPENDENCE

O*NET-SOC#	O*NET-SOC Title	O*NET-SOC#	O*NET-SOC Title
17-2021.00	Agricultural Engineers***	33-1021.02	Forest Fire Fighting and Prevention Supervisors
19-1011.00	Animal Scientists***	19-2043.00	Hydrologists***
19-2011.00	Astronomers***	17-2131.00	Materials Engineers***
19-1021.01	Biochemists***	19-1022.00	Microbiologists***
19-1021.02	Biophysicists***	53-5021.03	Pilots, Ship
27-2022.00	Coaches and Scouts***	19-1013.01	Plant Scientists***
17-2071.00	Electrical Engineers***	19-1031.02	Range Managers***
17-2072.00	Electronics Engineers, Except Computer***	19-1013.02	Soil Scientists***
11-9041.00	Engineering Managers***		

---

* Occupation included based on its highest interest area and second highest work value.
** Occupation included based on its highest interest area and third highest work value.
*** Occupation included based on its second highest interest area and highest work value.

REALISTIC — RECOGNITION

JOB ZONE 1 — REALISTIC — RECOGNITION

(No occupations for this combination in this job zone. To find occupations, look at other job zones in this combination or refer to the Interest and Work Value Master Lists.)

JOB ZONE 2 — REALISTIC — RECOGNITION

(No occupations for this combination in this job zone. To find occupations, look at other job zones in this combination or refer to the Interest and Work Value Master Lists.)

JOB ZONE 3 — REALISTIC — RECOGNITION

O*NET-SOC#	O*NET-SOC Title	O*NET-SOC#	O*NET-SOC Title
17-3012.01	Electronic Drafters**	37-1012.02	First-Line Supervisors and Manager/Supervisors - Landscaping Workers**
45-1011.06	First-Line Supervisors and Manager/Supervisors - Fishery Workers**	33-3031.00	Fish and Game Wardens**
45-1011.04	First-Line Supervisors and Manager/Supervisors - Horticultural Workers**	19-4041.02	Geological Sample Test Technicians**
		53-5021.02	Mates- Ship, Boat, and Barge

JOB ZONE 4 — REALISTIC — RECOGNITION

O*NET-SOC#	O*NET-SOC Title	O*NET-SOC#	O*NET-SOC Title
53-2011.00	Airline Pilots, Copilots, and Flight Engineers*	53-2012.00	Commercial Pilots*
17-2051.00	Civil Engineers**	27-2012.05	Technical Directors/Managers**

(To find more occupations, look at other job zones in this combination or refer to the Interest and Work Value Master Lists.)

JOB ZONE 5 — REALISTIC — RECOGNITION

O*NET-SOC#	O*NET-SOC Title	O*NET-SOC#	O*NET-SOC Title
33-1021.02	Forest Fire Fighting and Prevention Supervisors**	53-5021.03	Pilots, Ship**
17-2121.01	Marine Engineers**	53-5031.00	Ship Engineers**
17-2171.00	Petroleum Engineers**		

(To find more occupations, look at other job zones in this combination or refer to the Interest and Work Value Master Lists.)

* Occupation included based on its highest interest area and second highest work value.
** Occupation included based on its highest interest area and third highest work value.
*** Occupation included based on its second highest interest area and highest work value.

REALISTIC — RELATIONSHIPS

JOB ZONE 1 — REALISTIC — RELATIONSHIPS

O*NET-SOC#	O*NET-SOC Title	O*NET-SOC#	O*NET-SOC Title
39-3091.00	Amusement and Recreation Attendants	49-9098.00	Helpers—Installation, Maintenance, and Repair Workers
53-7061.00	Cleaners of Vehicles and Equipment		
35-3021.00	Combined Food Preparation and Serving Workers, Including Fast Food	47-3014.00	Helpers—Painters, Paperhangers, Plasterers, and Stucco Masons
35-2015.00	Cooks, Short Order	37-2011.00	Janitors and Cleaners, Except Maids and Housekeeping Cleaners
43-5021.00	Couriers and Messengers		
35-9011.00	Dining Room and Cafeteria Attendants and Bartender Helpers	37-3011.00	Landscaping and Groundskeeping Workers
		37-2012.00	Maids and Housekeeping Cleaners
35-9021.00	Dishwashers	53-6021.00	Parking Lot Attendants
45-2093.00	Farmworkers, Farm and Ranch Animals	51-6021.03	Pressers, Hand
45-3011.00	Fishers and Related Fishing Workers	51-9198.01	Production Laborers
35-2021.00	Food Preparation Workers	53-6031.00	Service Station Attendants
45-2092.02	General Farmworkers	51-6051.00	Sewers, Hand
47-3011.00	Helpers—Brickmasons, Blockmasons, Stonemasons, and Tile and Marble Setters	51-6011.01	Spotters, Dry Cleaning
		53-3041.00	Taxi Drivers and Chauffeurs
47-3012.00	Helpers—Carpenters	49-3093.00	Tire Repairers and Changers

JOB ZONE 2 — REALISTIC — RELATIONSHIPS

O*NET-SOC#	O*NET-SOC Titlel	O*NET-SOC#	O*NET-SOC Title
49-3091.00	Bicycle Repairers	47-2152.03	Pipelaying Fitters
35-2011.00	Cooks, Fast Food	51-6021.01	Pressers, Delicate Fabrics
35-2012.00	Cooks, Institution and Cafeteria	47-5051.00	Rock Splitters, Quarry
47-4031.00	Fence Erectors	37-3013.00	Tree Trimmers and Pruners
47-2043.00	Floor Sanders and Finishers	39-5091.00	Makeup Artists, Theatrical and Performance***
47-3015.00	Helpers—Pipelayers, Plumbers, Pipefitters, and Steamfitters	31-1012.00	Nursing Aides, Orderlies, and Attendants***
		31-2012.00	Occupational Therapist Aides***
33-9092.00	Lifeguards, Ski Patrol, and Other Recreational Protective Service Workers	31-2011.00	Occupational Therapist Assistants***
		39-9021.00	Personal and Home Care Aides***
47-2142.00	Paperhangers	29-2052.00	Pharmacy Technicians***
37-3012.00	Pesticide Handlers, Sprayers, and Applicators, Vegetation	31-2022.00	Physical Therapist Aides***
		31-2021.00	Physical Therapist Assistants***
47-2072.00	Pile-Driver Operators	31-1013.00	Psychiatric Aides***

JOB ZONE 3 — REALISTIC — RELATIONSHIPS

O*NET-SOC#	O*NET-SOC Title	O*NET-SOC#	O*NET-SOC Title
51-3011.01	Bakers, Bread and Pastry	29-2055.00	Surgical Technologists
39-5011.00	Barbers	47-2053.00	Terrazzo Workers and Finishers
51-3021.00	Butchers and Meat Cutters	31-9096.00	Veterinary Assistants and Laboratory Animal Caretakers
47-2051.00	Cement Masons and Concrete Finishers		
35-2014.00	Cooks, Restaurant	29-2031.00	Cardiovascular Technologists and Technicians***
47-2042.00	Floor Layers, Except Carpet, Wood, and Hard Tiles	31-9091.00	Dental Assistants***
47-2121.00	Glaziers	29-2061.00	Licensed Practical and Licensed Vocational Nurses***
49-9031.01	Home Appliance Installers		
47-2152.02	Plumbers	29-2053.00	Psychiatric Technicians***
47-2181.00	Roofers	29-1126.00	Respiratory Therapists***

---

* Occupation included based on its highest interest area and second highest work value.
** Occupation included based on its highest interest area and third highest work value.
*** Occupation included based on its second highest interest area and highest work value.

REALISTIC — RELATIONSHIPS (continued)

JOB ZONE 4 — REALISTIC — RELATIONSHIPS

O*NET-SOC#	O*NET-SOC Title	O*NET-SOC#	O*NET-SOC Title
47-2041.00	Carpet Installers	29-2034.02	Radiologic Technicians
39-4011.00	Embalmers	29-2051.00	Dietetic Technicians***
47-2141.00	Painters, Construction and Maintenance	29-1124.00	Radiation Therapists***
47-2161.00	Plasterers and Stucco Masons		

JOB ZONE 5 — REALISTIC — RELATIONSHIPS

O*NET-SOC#	O*NET-SOC Title
29-9091.00	Athletic Trainers***

(To find more occupations, look at other job zones in this combination or refer to the Interest and Work Value Master Lists.)

---

* Occupation included based on its highest interest area and second highest work value.
** Occupation included based on its highest interest area and third highest work value.
*** Occupation included based on its second highest interest area and highest work value.

REALISTIC — SUPPORT

JOB ZONE 1 — REALISTIC — SUPPORT

O*NET-SOC#	O*NET-SOC Title	O*NET-SOC#	O*NET-SOC Title
51-5011.02	Bindery Machine Operators and Tenders	51-4072.04	Metal Molding, Coremaking, and Casting Machine Operators and Tenders
53-3021.00	Bus Drivers, Transit and Intercity		
51-9191.00	Cementing and Gluing Machine Operators and Tenders	51-9023.00	Mixing and Blending Machine Setters, Operators, and Tenders
51-9192.00	Cleaning, Washing, and Metal Pickling Equipment Operators and Tenders	51-4193.04	Nonelectrolytic Plating and Coating Machine Operators and Tenders, Metal and Plastic
51-9121.02	Coating, Painting, and Spraying Machine Operators and Tenders	39-2021.00	Nonfarm Animal Caretakers
53-7011.00	Conveyor Operators and Tenders	45-2092.01	Nursery Workers
51-9193.00	Cooling and Freezing Equipment Operators and Tenders	51-9111.00	Packaging and Filling Machine Operators and Tenders
51-9021.00	Crushing, Grinding, and Polishing Machine Setters, Operators, and Tenders	53-7064.00	Packers and Packagers, Hand
		51-9123.00	Painting, Coating, and Decorating Workers
51-9031.00	Cutters and Trimmers, Hand	51-9194.04	Pantograph Engravers
51-9032.04	Cutting and Slicing Machine Operators and Tenders	51-4072.04	Plastic Molding and Casting Machine Operators and Tenders
51-9194.05	Etchers, Hand	51-4052.00	Pourers and Casters, Metal
51-6091.01	Extruding and Forming Machine Operators and Tenders, Synthetic or Glass Fibers	51-6021.02	Pressing Machine Operators and Tenders- Textile, Garment, and Related Materials
51-9041.02	Extruding, Forming, Pressing, and Compacting Machine Operators and Tenders	51-5023.09	Printing Press Machine Operators and Tenders
		51-9198.02	Production Helpers
49-9093.00	Fabric Menders, Except Garment	51-9061.05	Production Inspectors, Testers, Graders, Sorters, Samplers, Weighers
45-4021.00	Fallers		
51-3091.00	Food and Tobacco Roasting, Baking, and Drying Machine Operators and Tenders	47-4061.00	Rail-Track Laying and Maintenance Equipment Operators
51-3093.00	Food Cooking Machine Operators and Tenders	53-4021.02	Railroad Yard Workers
53-7062.03	Freight, Stock, and Material Movers, Hand	49-9045.00	Refractory Materials Repairers, Except Brickmasons
51-9051.00	Furnace, Kiln, Oven, Drier, and Kettle Operators and Tenders	53-7081.00	Refuse and Recyclable Material Collectors
		51-9141.00	Semiconductor Processors
51-9032.03	Glass Cutting Machine Setters and Set-Up Operators	51-9012.00	Separating, Filtering, Clarifying, Precipitating, and Still Machine Setters, Operators, and Tenders
45-2041.00	Graders and Sorters, Agricultural Products	51-6031.01	Sewing Machine Operators, Garment
51-9022.00	Grinding and Polishing Workers, Hand	51-6031.02	Sewing Machine Operators, Non-Garment
47-5081.00	Helpers—Extraction Workers	51-6042.00	Shoe Machine Operators and Tenders
49-9098.00	Helpers—Installation, Maintenance, and Repair Workers	51-4121.04	Solderers
		51-4122.04	Soldering and Brazing Machine Operators and Tenders
47-4051.00	Highway Maintenance Workers	53-7062.01	Stevedores, Except Equipment Operators
53-7041.00	Hoist and Winch Operators	43-5081.01	Stock Clerks, Sales Floor
53-7051.00	Industrial Truck and Tractor Operators	51-6061.00	Textile Bleaching and Dyeing Machine Operators and Tenders
51-6011.03	Laundry and Drycleaning Machine Operators and Tenders, Except Pressing		
53-7063.00	Machine Feeders and Offbearers	51-9197.00	Tire Builders
43-9051.01	Mail Machine Operators, Preparation and Handling	53-3033.00	Truck Drivers, Light or Delivery Services
49-9043.00	Maintenance Workers, Machinery	51-4121.01	Welders, Production
51-5023.05	Marking and Identification Printing Machine Setters and Set-Up Operators	51-7042.02	Woodworking Machine Operators and Tenders, Except Sawing
51-3022.00	Meat, Poultry, and Fish Cutters and Trimmers		

* Occupation included based on its highest interest area and second highest work value.
** Occupation included based on its highest interest area and third highest work value.
*** Occupation included based on its second highest interest area and highest work value.

REALISTIC — SUPPORT (continued)

JOB ZONE 2 — REALISTIC — SUPPORT

O*NET-SOC#	O*NET-SOC Title	O*NET-SOC#	O*NET-SOC Title
53-5011.01	Able Seamen	47-4041.01	Irradiated-Fuel Handlers
19-4011.01	Agricultural Technicians	53-7033.00	Loading Machine Operators, Underground Mining
49-3022.00	Automotive Glass Installers and Repairers	45-4023.00	Log Graders and Scalers
51-8013.02	Auxiliary Equipment Operators, Power	45-4022.01	Logging Tractor Operators
49-2092.03	Battery Repairers	49-9095.00	Manufactured Building and Mobile Home Installers
51-5011.01	Bindery Machine Setters and Set-Up Operators	31-9093.00	Medical Equipment Preparers
19-4021.00	Biological Technicians	51-4051.00	Metal-Refining Furnace Operators and Tenders
51-8021.01	Boiler Operators and Tenders, Low Pressure	51-4072.03	Metal Molding, Coremaking, and Casting Machine Setters and Set-Up Operators
47-2031.06	Brattice Builders		
51-4121.05	Brazers	49-9012.03	Meter Mechanics
53-6011.00	Bridge and Lock Tenders	47-5042.00	Mine Cutting and Channeling Machine Operators
51-4033.02	Buffing and Polishing Set-Up Operators	51-9195.06	Mold Makers, Hand
53-3022.00	Bus Drivers, School	51-9195.07	Molding and Casting Workers
51-9011.01	Chemical Equipment Controllers and Operators	39-3021.00	Motion Picture Projectionists
51-9011.02	Chemical Equipment Tenders	53-6051.05	Motor Vehicle Inspectors
51-8091.00	Chemical Plant and System Operators	51-4011.01	Numerical Control Machine Tool Operators and Tenders, Metal and Plastic
51-9121.01	Coating, Painting, and Spraying Machine Setters and Set-Up Operators		
		53-5011.02	Ordinary Seamen and Marine Oilers
51-2021.00	Coil Winders, Tapers, and Finishers	51-9122.00	Painters, Transportation Equipment
51-4081.02	Combination Machine Tool Operators and Tenders, Metal and Plastic	51-9196.00	Paper Goods Machine Setters, Operators, and Tenders
47-5021.01	Construction Drillers	47-2071.00	Paving, Surfacing, and Tamping Equipment Operators
47-2061.00	Construction Laborers		
47-5041.00	Continuous Mining Machine Operators	37-2021.00	Pest Control Workers
33-3012.00	Correctional Officers and Jailers	51-5022.13	Photoengraving and Lithographing Machine Operators and Tenders
53-7021.00	Crane and Tower Operators		
47-5011.00	Derrick Operators, Oil and Gas	51-9132.00	Photographic Processing Machine Operators
53-7032.02	Dragline Operators	47-2151.00	Pipelayers
53-7031.00	Dredge Operators	51-4072.01	Plastic Molding and Casting Machine Setters and Set-Up Operators
51-4032.00	Drilling and Boring Machine Tool Setters, Operators, and Tenders, Metal and Plastic		
		51-5023.01	Precision Printing Workers
47-2081.02	Drywall Installers	51-4031.03	Press and Press Brake Machine Setters and Set-Up Operators, Metal and Plastic
49-2092.05	Electrical Parts Reconditioners		
51-4193.02	Electrolytic Plating and Coating Machine Operators and Tenders, Metal and Plastic	53-7072.00	Pump Operators, Except Wellhead Pumpers
		51-4031.02	Punching Machine Setters and Set-Up Operators, Metal and Plastic
53-7032.01	Excavating and Loading Machine Operators		
47-5031.00	Explosives Workers, Ordnance Handling Experts, and Blasters	53-4013.00	Rail Yard Engineers, Dinkey Operators, and Hostlers
		53-6051.04	Railroad Inspectors
51-4021.00	Extruding and Drawing Machine Setters, Operators, and Tenders, Metal and Plastic	49-3092.00	Recreational Vehicle Service Technicians
		51-4023.00	Rolling Machine Setters, Operators, and Tenders, Metal and Plastic
51-9041.01	Extruding, Forming, Pressing, and Compacting Machine Setters and Set-Up Operators		
		47-5061.00	Roof Bolters, Mining
51-9032.01	Fiber Product Cutting Machine Setters and Set-Up Operators	47-5071.00	Roustabouts, Oil and Gas
		51-7041.02	Sawing Machine Operators and Tenders
51-4022.00	Forging Machine Setters, Operators, and Tenders, Metal and Plastic	51-7041.01	Sawing Machine Setters and Set-Up Operators
		51-4031.01	Sawing Machine Tool Setters and Set-Up Operators, Metal and Plastic
51-4071.00	Foundry Mold and Coremakers		
49-2022.02	Frame Wirers, Central Office	47-4071.00	Septic Tank Servicers and Sewer Pipe Cleaners
51-8092.01	Gas Processing Plant Operators	51-4031.04	Shear and Slitter Machine Setters and Set-Up Operators, Metal and Plastic
53-7071.01	Gas Pumping Station Operators		
47-2073.01	Grader, Bulldozer, and Scraper Operators	53-7111.00	Shuttle Car Operators
53-7062.02	Grips and Set-Up Workers, Motion Picture Sets, Studios, and Stages	51-3023.00	Slaughterers and Meat Packers
		51-4122.03	Soldering and Brazing Machine Setters and Set-Up Operators
51-4191.02	Heat Treating, Annealing, and Tempering Machine Operators and Tenders, Metal and Plastic		
		53-4041.00	Stone Sawyers
		53-4041.00	Subway and Streetcar Operators
51-4191.03	Heaters, Metal and Plastic	51-9032.02	Stone Sawyers
47-3013.00	Helpers—Electricians	47-2082.00	Tapers

---

* Occupation included based on its highest interest area and second highest work value.
** Occupation included based on its highest interest area and third highest work value.
*** Occupation included based on its second highest interest area and highest work value.

REALISTIC — SUPPORT (continued)

JOB ZONE 2 — REALISTIC — SUPPORT (CONTINUED)

O*NET-SOC#	O*NET-SOC Title	O*NET-SOC#	O*NET-SOC Title
53-3032.02	Tractor-Trailer Truck Drivers	51-4121.02	Welders and Cutters
53-4021.01	Train Crew Members	51-4122.02	Welding Machine Operators and Tenders
51-5022.12	Typesetting and Composing Machine Operators and Tenders	51-7042.01	Woodworking Machine Setters and Set-Up Operators, Except Sawing
51-8031.00	Water and Liquid Waste Treatment Plant and System Operators		

JOB ZONE 3 — REALISTIC — SUPPORT

O*NET-SOC#	O*NET-SOC Title	O*NET-SOC#	O*NET-SOC Title
51-2011.03	Aircraft Rigging Assemblers	51-5023.03	Letterpress Setters and Set-Up Operators
51-2011.01	Aircraft Structure Assemblers, Precision	53-4012.00	Locomotive Firers
51-2011.02	Aircraft Systems Assemblers, Precision	49-9042.00	Maintenance and Repair Workers, General
49-2011.01	Automatic Teller Machine Servicers	51-9061.01	Materials Inspectors
51-3011.01	Bakers, Bread and Pastry	53-5021.02	Mates- Ship, Boat, and Barge
51-3011.02	Bakers, Manufacturing	49-9011.00	Mechanical Door Repairers
51-4072.05	Casting Machine Set-Up Operators	51-4035.00	Milling and Planing Machine Setters, Operators, and Tenders, Metal and Plastic
51-4081.01	Combination Machine Tool Setters and Set-Up Operators, Metal and Plastic	51-4193.03	Nonelectrolytic Plating and Coating Machine Setters and Set-Up Operators, Metal and Plastic
49-2022.03	Communication Equipment Mechanics, Installers, and Repairers	19-4051.01	Nuclear Equipment Operation Technicians
51-5023.04	Design Printing Machine Setters and Set-Up Operators	19-4051.02	Nuclear Monitoring Technicians
		49-2011.03	Office Machine and Cash Register Servicers
49-9012.01	Electric Meter Installers and Repairers	47-2073.02	Operating Engineers
51-2022.00	Electrical and Electronic Equipment Assemblers	51-8093.01	Petroleum Pump System Operators
51-9061.04	Electrical and Electronic Inspectors and Testers	51-9061.03	Precision Devices Inspectors and Testers
49-2093.00	Electrical and Electronics Installers and Repairers, Transportation Equipment	51-6011.02	Precision Dyers
		51-9195.01	Precision Mold and Pattern Casters, except Nonferrous Metals
51-4193.01	Electrolytic Plating and Coating Machine Setters and Set-Up Operators, Metal and Plastic	47-2171.00	Reinforcing Iron and Rebar Workers
51-2023.00	Electromechanical Equipment Assemblers	49-9096.00	Riggers
49-2096.00	Electronic Equipment Installers and Repairers, Motor Vehicles	47-5012.00	Rotary Drill Operators, Oil and Gas
		51-5023.06	Screen Printing Machine Setters and Set-Up Operators
51-5023.07	Embossing Machine Set-Up Operators	47-2211.00	Sheet Metal Workers
51-2031.00	Engine and Other Machine Assemblers	51-8021.02	Stationary Engineers
51-9194.06	Engravers, Hand	47-2221.00	Structural Iron and Steel Workers
51-3092.00	Food Batchmakers	53-7121.00	Tank Car, Truck, and Ship Loaders
51-8092.02	Gas Distribution Plant Operators	49-2022.04	Telecommunications Facility Examiners
51-8093.03	Gaugers	49-9052.00	Telecommunications Line Installers and Repairers
19-4041.01	Geological Data Technicians	51-6062.00	Textile Cutting Machine Setters, Operators, and Tenders
19-4041.02	Geological Sample Test Technicians	51-6063.00	Textile Knitting and Weaving Machine Setters, Operators, and Tenders
51-4033.01	Grinding, Honing, Lapping, and Deburring Machine Set-Up Operators		
51-4191.01	Heating Equipment Setters and Set-Up Operators, Metal and Plastic	51-6064.00	Textile Winding, Twisting, and Drawing Out Machine Setters, Operators, and Tenders
47-2131.00	Insulation Workers, Floor, Ceiling, and Wall	51-4194.00	Tool Grinders, Filers, and Sharpeners
47-2132.00	Insulation Workers, Mechanical	49-9012.02	Valve and Regulator Repairers
51-4034.00	Lathe and Turning Machine Tool Setters, Operators, and Tenders, Metal and Plastic	51-4122.01	Welding Machine Setters and Set-Up Operators
51-4192.00	Lay-Out Workers, Metal and Plastic	47-5021.02	Well and Core Drill Operators

---

* Occupation included based on its highest interest area and second highest work value.
** Occupation included based on its highest interest area and third highest work value.
*** Occupation included based on its second highest interest area and highest work value.

REALISTIC — SUPPORT (continued)

JOB ZONE 4 — REALISTIC — SUPPORT

O*NET-SOC#	O*NET-SOC Title	O*NET-SOC#	O*NET-SOC Title
53-6051.01	Aviation Inspectors	51-9083.02	Optical Instrument Assemblers
49-2091.00	Avionics Technicians	51-4062.00	Patternmakers, Metal and Plastic
47-2011.00	Boilermakers	51-8093.02	Petroleum Refinery and Control Panel Operators
51-5012.00	Bookbinders	51-8012.00	Power Distributors and Dispatchers
17-3023.02	Calibration and Instrumentation Technicians	51-8013.01	Power Generating Plant Operators, Except Auxiliary Equipment Operators
47-2081.01	Ceiling Tile Installers		
49-2022.01	Central Office and PBX Installers and Repairers	51-9195.02	Precision Pattern and Die Casters, Nonferrous Metals
49-9051.00	Electrical Power-Line Installers and Repairers		
17-3024.00	Electro-Mechanical Technicians	13-1041.05	Pressure Vessel Inspectors
47-4021.00	Elevator Installers and Repairers	53-4031.00	Railroad Conductors and Yardmasters
51-5023.08	Engraver Set-Up Operators	49-9021.02	Refrigeration Mechanics
51-2041.02	Fitters, Structural Metal- Precision	47-5013.00	Service Unit Operators, Oil, Gas, and Mining
49-9031.02	Gas Appliance Repairers	49-9097.00	Signal and Track Switch Repairers
53-7071.02	Gas Compressor Operators	49-2022.05	Station Installers and Repairers, Telephone
51-5022.01	Hand Compositors and Typesetters	17-3031.01	Surveying Technicians
53-4011.00	Locomotive Engineers	51-4111.00	Tool and Die Makers
51-4041.00	Machinists	53-6041.00	Traffic Technicians
51-9061.02	Mechanical Inspectors	49-2092.04	Transformer Repairers
51-2041.01	Metal Fabricators, Structural Metal Products	51-4121.03	Welder-Fitters
49-9044.00	Millwrights	53-7073.00	Wellhead Pumpers
51-8011.00	Nuclear Power Reactor Operators		

JOB ZONE 5 — REALISTIC — SUPPORT

O*NET-SOC#	O*NET-SOC Title	O*NET-SOC#	O*NET-SOC Title
49-2095.00	Electrical and Electronics Repairers, Powerhouse, Substation, and Relay	51-5023.02	Offset Lithographic Press Setters and Set-Up Operators
51-5022.10	Electrotypers and Stereotypers	51-5022.11	Plate Finishers
53-6051.03	Marine Cargo Inspectors***		

(To find more occupations, look at other job zones in this combination or refer to the Interest and Work Value Master Lists.)

---

* Occupation included based on its highest interest area and second highest work value.
** Occupation included based on its highest interest area and third highest work value.
*** Occupation included based on its second highest interest area and highest work value.

REALISTIC — WORKING CONDITIONS

JOB ZONE 1 — REALISTIC — WORKING CONDITIONS

O*NET-SOC#	O*NET-SOC Title	O*NET-SOC#	O*NET-SOC Title
51-5011.02	Bindery Machine Operators and Tenders*	51-9141.00	Semiconductor Processors*
53-3021.00	Bus Drivers, Transit and Intercity*	51-6031.01	Sewing Machine Operators, Garment*
49-9043.00	Maintenance Workers, Machinery*	51-6031.02	Sewing Machine Operators, Non-Garment*
51-9061.05	Production Inspectors, Testers, Graders, Sorters, Samplers, Weighers*	53-3032.01	Truck Drivers, Heavy
49-9045.00	Refractory Materials Repairers, Except Brickmasons*	53-3033.00	Truck Drivers, Light or Delivery Services*

JOB ZONE 2 — REALISTIC — WORKING CONDITIONS

O*NET-SOC#	O*NET-SOC Title	O*NET-SOC#	O*NET-SOC Title
51-8091.00	Chemical Plant and System Operators*	51-9071.06	Gem and Diamond Workers*
49-9091.00	Coin, Vending, and Amusement Machine Servicers and Repairers	49-2092.06	Hand and Portable Power Tool Repairers
19-4011.02	Food Science Technicians	51-9082.00	Medical Appliance Technicians*
51-7021.00	Furniture Finishers	51-9131.03	Photographic Hand Developers
		51-5023.01	Precision Printing Workers*

JOB ZONE 3 — REALISTIC — WORKING CONDITIONS

O*NET-SOC#	O*NET-SOC Title	O*NET-SOC#	O*NET-SOC Title
51-9071.04	Bench Workers, Jewelry	49-9062.00	Medical Equipment Repairers
51-9081.00	Dental Laboratory Technicians	51-9071.03	Model and Mold Makers, Jewelry
49-2092.01	Electric Home Appliance and Power Tool Repairers	51-4012.00	Numerical Tool and Process Control Programmers
49-2092.02	Electric Motor and Switch Assemblers and Repairers	49-9063.04	Percussion Instrument Repairers and Tuners
49-2097.00	Electronic Home Entertainment Equipment Installers and Repairers	51-9131.02	Photographic Reproduction Technicians
		51-9083.01	Precision Lens Grinders and Polishers
19-4091.00	Environmental Science and Protection Technicians, Including Health***	49-2021.00	Radio Mechanics
49-9041.00	Industrial Machinery Mechanics	47-2031.04	Ship Carpenters and Joiners
49-9063.01	Keyboard Instrument Repairers and Tuners	51-6052.01	Shop and Alteration Tailors
49-9094.00	Locksmiths and Safe Repairers	49-9063.02	Stringed Instrument Repairers and Tuners
		49-9064.00	Watch Repairers

* Occupation included based on its highest interest area and second highest work value.
** Occupation included based on its highest interest area and third highest work value.
*** Occupation included based on its second highest interest area and highest work value.

REALISTIC — WORKING CONDITIONS (continued)

JOB ZONE 4 — REALISTIC — WORKING CONDITIONS

O*NET-SOC#	O*NET-SOC Title	O*NET-SOC#	O*NET-SOC Title
45-2011.00	Agricultural Inspectors	51-9131.04	Film Laboratory Technicians
49-9061.00	Camera and Photographic Equipment Repairers	49-9021.01	Heating and Air Conditioning Mechanics
49-2011.02	Data Processing Equipment Repairers	51-5022.02	Paste-Up Workers
43-9031.00	Desktop Publishers	49-9063.03	Reed or Wind Instrument Repairers and Tuners
51-5022.09	Electronic Masking System Operators	51-5022.05	Scanner Operators

JOB ZONE 5 — REALISTIC — WORKING CONDITIONS

O*NET-SOC#	O*NET-SOC Title	O*NET-SOC#	O*NET-SOC Title
51-5022.08	Dot Etchers	51-5021.00	Job Printers
49-2095.00	Electrical and Electronics Repairers, Powerhouse, Substation, and Relay*	51-5023.02	Offset Lithographic Press Setters and Set-Up Operators*
51-5022.10	Electrotypers and Stereotypers*	51-5022.11	Plate Finishers*

* Occupation included based on its highest interest area and second highest work value.
** Occupation included based on its highest interest area and third highest work value.
*** Occupation included based on its second highest interest area and highest work value.

INVESTIGATIVE

INVESTIGATIVE — ACHIEVEMENT

JOB ZONE 1 — INVESTIGATIVE — ACHIEVEMENT

O*NET-SOC#	O*NET-SOC Title
45-4011.00	Forest and Conservation Workers***

(To find more occupations, look at other job zones in this combination or refer to the Interest and Work Value Master Lists.)

JOB ZONE 2 — INVESTIGATIVE — ACHIEVEMENT

O*NET-SOC#	O*NET-SOC Title
29-2012.00	Medical and Clinical Laboratory Technicians***
51-9082.00	Medical Appliance Technicians***

(To find more occupations, look at other job zones in this combination or refer to the Interest and Work Value Master Lists.)

JOB ZONE 3 — INVESTIGATIVE — ACHIEVEMENT

O*NET-SOC#	O*NET-SOC Title	O*NET-SOC#	O*NET-SOC Title
19-4031.00	Chemical Technicians***	13-1041.01	Environmental Compliance Inspectors
13-1072.00	Compensation, Benefits, and Job Analysis Specialists	17-3026.00	Industrial Engineering Technicians
49-2094.00	Electrical and Electronics Repairers, Commercial and Industrial Equipment***	13-1031.02	Insurance Adjusters, Examiners, and Investigators***
		49-3051.00	Motorboat Mechanics***
47-2111.00	Electricians***	29-2091.00	Orthotists and Prosthetists***

JOB ZONE 4 — INVESTIGATIVE — ACHIEVEMENT

O*NET-SOC#	O*NET-SOC Title	O*NET-SOC#	O*NET-SOC Title
17-3021.00	Aerospace Engineering and Operations Technicians	19-3021.00	Market Research Analysts
19-2021.00	Atmospheric and Space Scientists	15-3011.00	Mathematical Technicians
19-2031.00	Chemists	29-2011.00	Medical and Clinical Laboratory Technologists
17-2061.00	Computer Hardware Engineers	19-1042.00	Medical Scientists, Except Epidemiologists
15-1021.00	Computer Programmers	15-1081.00	Network Systems and Data Communications Analysts
15-1031.00	Computer Software Engineers, Applications		
15-1032.00	Computer Software Engineers, Systems Software	29-2033.00	Nuclear Medicine Technologists
15-1041.00	Computer Support Specialists	29-1041.00	Optometrists
29-1031.00	Dietitians and Nutritionists	29-1051.00	Pharmacists
19-3031.01	Educational Psychologists	29-1071.00	Physician Assistants
19-1041.00	Epidemiologists	15-2041.00	Statisticians
33-2021.02	Fire Investigators	17-1022.00	Surveyors
19-4092.00	Forensic Science Technicians	19-3051.00	Urban and Regional Planners

---

* Occupation included based on its highest interest area and second highest work value.
** Occupation included based on its highest interest area and third highest work value.
*** Occupation included based on its second highest interest area and highest work value.

INVESTIGATIVE — ACHIEVEMENT (continued)

JOB ZONE 5 — INVESTIGATIVE — ACHIEVEMENT

O*NET-SOC#	O*NET-SOC Title	O*NET-SOC#	O*NET-SOC Title
17-2011.00	Aerospace Engineers	19-2042.01	Geologists
25-1041.00	Agricultural Sciences Teachers, Postsecondary	25-1071.00	Health Specialties Teachers, Postsecondary
29-1061.00	Anesthesiologists	29-1063.00	Internists, General
25-4011.00	Archivists	25-1022.00	Mathematical Science Teachers, Postsecondary
25-1042.00	Biological Science Teachers, Postsecondary	15-2021.00	Mathematicians
19-1020.01	Biologists	17-2161.00	Nuclear Engineers
17-2041.00	Chemical Engineers	29-1064.00	Obstetricians and Gynecologists
25-1052.00	Chemistry Teachers, Postsecondary	29-1022.00	Oral and Maxillofacial Surgeons
29-1011.00	Chiropractors	29-1023.00	Orthodontists
25-1021.00	Computer Science Teachers, Postsecondary	29-1065.00	Pediatricians, General
29-1021.00	Dentists, General	19-2012.00	Physicists
19-3011.00	Economists	25-1054.00	Physics Teachers, Postsecondary
25-1032.00	Engineering Teachers, Postsecondary	17-2111.03	Product Safety Engineers
19-2041.00	Environmental Scientists and Specialists, Including Health	29-1024.00	Prosthodontists
		29-1066.00	Psychiatrists
29-1062.00	Family and General Practitioners	29-1067.00	Surgeons
25-1043.00	Forestry and Conservation Science Teachers, Postsecondary	29-1131.00	Veterinarians
		19-1023.00	Zoologists and Wildlife Biologists

* Occupation included based on its highest interest area and second highest work value.
** Occupation included based on its highest interest area and third highest work value.
*** Occupation included based on its second highest interest area and highest work value.

INVESTIGATIVE — INDEPENDENCE

JOB ZONE 1 — INVESTIGATIVE — INDEPENDENCE

(No occupations for this combination in this job zone. To find occupations, look at other job zones in this combination or refer to the Interest and Work Value Master Lists.)

JOB ZONE 2 — INVESTIGATIVE — INDEPENDENCE

(No occupations for this combination in this job zone. To find occupations, look at other job zones in this combination or refer to the Interest and Work Value Master Lists.)

JOB ZONE 3 — INVESTIGATIVE — INDEPENDENCE

O*NET-SOC#	O*NET-SOC Title	O*NET-SOC#	O*NET-SOC Title
45-2021.00	Animal Breeders***	33-3031.00	Fish and Game Wardens***
15-1051.00	Computer Systems Analysts	19-3041.00	Sociologists

(To find more occupations, look at other job zones in this combination or refer to the Interest and Work Value Master Lists.)

JOB ZONE 4 — INVESTIGATIVE — INDEPENDENCE

O*NET-SOC#	O*NET-SOC Title	O*NET-SOC#	O*NET-SOC Title
19-3091.01	Anthropologists	19-3092.00	Geographers
19-3091.02	Archeologists	19-3093.00	Historians
19-3031.02	Clinical Psychologists	17-2112.00	Industrial Engineers***
15-1071.01	Computer Security Specialists	17-2111.01	Industrial Safety and Health Engineers
13-1041.06	Coroners	19-2032.00	Materials Scientists
25-4012.00	Curators***	17-2141.00	Mechanical Engineers***
15-1061.00	Database Administrators	17-2151.00	Mining and Geological Engineers, Including
17-2111.02	Fire-Prevention and Protection Engineers		Mining Safety Engineers
19-1012.00	Food Scientists and Technologists	15-2031.00	Operations Research Analysts
19-1032.00	Foresters***	19-1031.01	Soil Conservationists

JOB ZONE 5 — INVESTIGATIVE — INDEPENDENCE

O*NET-SOC#	O*NET-SOC Title	O*NET-SOC#	O*NET-SOC Title
17-2021.00	Agricultural Engineers	19-3032.00	Industrial-Organizational Psychologists
19-1011.00	Animal Scientists	25-9031.00	Instructional Coordinators***
19-2011.00	Astronomers	17-2131.00	Materials Engineers
19-1021.01	Biochemists	19-1022.00	Microbiologists
19-1021.02	Biophysicists	11-9121.00	Natural Sciences Managers
17-2071.00	Electrical Engineers	19-1013.01	Plant Scientists
17-2072.00	Electronics Engineers, Except Computer	19-3094.00	Political Scientists
13-2051.00	Financial Analysts	19-1031.02	Range Managers
19-2043.00	Hydrologists	19-1013.02	Soil Scientists

* Occupation included based on its highest interest area and second highest work value.
** Occupation included based on its highest interest area and third highest work value.
*** Occupation included based on its second highest interest area and highest work value.

INVESTIGATIVE — RECOGNITION

JOB ZONE 1 — INVESTIGATIVE — RECOGNITION

(No occupations for this combination in this job zone. To find occupations, look at other job zones in this combination or refer to the Interest and Work Value Master Lists.)

JOB ZONE 2 — INVESTIGATIVE — RECOGNITION

(No occupations for this combination in this job zone. To find occupations, look at other job zones in this combination or refer to the Interest and Work Value Master Lists.)

JOB ZONE 3 — INVESTIGATIVE — RECOGNITION

(No occupations for this combination in this job zone. To find occupations, look at other job zones in this combination or refer to the Interest and Work Value Master Lists.)

JOB ZONE 4 — INVESTIGATIVE — RECOGNITION

O*NET-SOC#	O*NET-SOC Title
17-2151.00	Mining and Geological Engineers, Including Mining Safety Engineers**

(To find more occupations, look at other job zones in this combination or refer to the Interest and Work Value Master Lists.)

JOB ZONE 5 — INVESTIGATIVE — RECOGNITION

O*NET-SOC#	O*NET-SOC Title	O*NET-SOC#	O*NET-SOC Title
17-2011.00	Aerospace Engineers**	29-1067.00	Surgeons**
17-2041.00	Chemical Engineers**		

(To find more occupations, look at other job zones in this combination or refer to the Interest and Work Value Master Lists.)

* Occupation included based on its highest interest area and second highest work value.
** Occupation included based on its highest interest area and third highest work value.
*** Occupation included based on its second highest interest area and highest work value.

INVESTIGATIVE — RELATIONSHIPS

JOB ZONE 1 — INVESTIGATIVE — RELATIONSHIPS

(No occupations for this combination in this job zone. To find occupations, look at other job zones in this combination or refer to the Interest and Work Value Master Lists.)

JOB ZONE 2 — INVESTIGATIVE — RELATIONSHIPS

(No occupations for this combination in this job zone. To find occupations, look at other job zones in this combination or refer to the Interest and Work Value Master Lists.)

JOB ZONE 3 — INVESTIGATIVE — RELATIONSHIPS

O*NET-SOC#	O*NET-SOC Title
29-2031.00	Cardiovascular Technologists and Technicians
29-1126.00	Respiratory Therapists

(To find more occupations, look at other job zones in this combination or refer to the Interest and Work Value Master Lists.)

JOB ZONE 4 — INVESTIGATIVE — RELATIONSHIPS

O*NET-SOC#	O*NET-SOC Title
29-1031.00	Dietitians and Nutritionists*
29-1071.00	Physician Assistants*

(To find more occupations, look at other job zones in this combination or refer to the Interest and Work Value Master Lists.)

JOB ZONE 5 — INVESTIGATIVE — RELATIONSHIPS

O*NET-SOC#	O*NET-SOC Title	O*NET-SOC#	O*NET-SOC Title
25-1041.00	Agricultural Sciences Teachers, Postsecondary**	25-1191.00	Graduate Teaching Assistants***
29-1061.00	Anesthesiologists*	25-1071.00	Health Specialties Teachers, Postsecondary**
25-1042.00	Biological Science Teachers, Postsecondary**	29-1063.00	Internists, General**
25-1052.00	Chemistry Teachers, Postsecondary**	29-1064.00	Obstetricians and Gynecologists**
29-1021.00	Dentists, General**	29-1022.00	Oral and Maxillofacial Surgeons**
29-1062.00	Family and General Practitioners**	29-1023.00	Orthodontists**
25-1043.00	Forestry and Conservation Science Teachers, Postsecondary**	29-1065.00	Pediatricians, General**
		25-1054.00	Physics Teachers, Postsecondary**

* Occupation included based on its highest interest area and second highest work value.
** Occupation included based on its highest interest area and third highest work value.
*** Occupation included based on its second highest interest area and highest work value.

INVESTIGATIVE — SUPPORT

JOB ZONE 1 — INVESTIGATIVE — SUPPORT

(No occupations for this combination in this job zone. To find occupations, look at other job zones in this combination or refer to the Interest and Work Value Master Lists.)

JOB ZONE 2 — INVESTIGATIVE — SUPPORT

O*NET-SOC#	O*NET-SOC Title
19-4011.01	Agricultural Technicians***
19-4021.00	Biological Technicians***

(To find more occupations, look at other job zones in this combination or refer to the Interest and Work Value Master Lists.)

JOB ZONE 3 — INVESTIGATIVE — SUPPORT

O*NET-SOC#	O*NET-SOC Title	O*NET-SOC#	O*NET-SOC Title
19-4061.01	City Planning Aides***	47-2073.02	Operating Engineers***
19-4041.02	Geological Sample Test Technicians***	51-6011.02	Precision Dyers***
19-4051.01	Nuclear Equipment Operation Technicians***	49-2022.04	Telecommunications Facility Examiners***
19-4051.02	Nuclear Monitoring Technicians***		

JOB ZONE 4 — INVESTIGATIVE — SUPPORT

O*NET-SOC#	O*NET-SOC Title	O*NET-SOC#	O*NET-SOC Title
53-6051.01	Aviation Inspectors***	49-9044.00	Millwrights***
49-2091.00	Avionics Technicians***	51-8093.02	Petroleum Refinery and Control Panel Operators***
49-2022.01	Central Office and PBX Installers and Repairers***	53-6041.00	Traffic Technicians***
17-3024.00	Electro-Mechanical Technicians***	51-4121.03	Welder-Fitters***
51-4041.00	Machinists***		

JOB ZONE 5 — INVESTIGATIVE — SUPPORT

O*NET-SOC#	O*NET-SOC Title
49-2095.00	Electrical and Electronics Repairers, Powerhouse, Substation, and Relay***

(To find more occupations, look at other job zones in this combination or refer to the Interest and Work Value Master Lists.)

* Occupation included based on its highest interest area and second highest work value.
** Occupation included based on its highest interest area and third highest work value.
*** Occupation included based on its second highest interest area and highest work value.

INVESTIGATIVE — WORKING CONDITIONS

JOB ZONE 1 — INVESTIGATIVE — WORKING CONDITIONS

(No occupations for this combination in this job zone. To find occupations, look at other job zones in this combination or refer to the Interest and Work Value Master Lists.)

JOB ZONE 2 — INVESTIGATIVE — WORKING CONDITIONS

O*NET-SOC#	O*NET-SOC Title
19-4011.02	Food Science Technicians***

(To find more occupations, look at other job zones in this combination or refer to the Interest and Work Value Master Lists.)

JOB ZONE 3 — INVESTIGATIVE — WORKING CONDITIONS

O*NET-SOC#	O*NET-SOC Title	O*NET-SOC#	O*NET-SOC Title
51-9081.00	Dental Laboratory Technicians***	49-9062.00	Medical Equipment Repairers***
19-4091.00	Environmental Science and Protection Technicians, Including Health		

(To find more occupations, look at other job zones in this combination or refer to the Interest and Work Value Master Lists.)

JOB ZONE 4 — INVESTIGATIVE — WORKING CONDITIONS

O*NET-SOC#	O*NET-SOC Title
45-2011.00	Agricultural Inspectors***

(To find more occupations, look at other job zones in this combination or refer to the Interest and Work Value Master Lists.)

JOB ZONE 5 — INVESTIGATIVE — WORKING CONDITIONS

O*NET-SOC#	O*NET-SOC Title	O*NET-SOC#	O*NET-SOC Title
15-2011.00	Actuaries***	19-2012.00	Physicists**
19-1021.01	Biochemists**	29-1066.00	Psychiatrists**
19-1021.02	Biophysicists**	29-1131.00	Veterinarians**
29-1011.00	Chiropractors**		

---

* Occupation included based on its highest interest area and second highest work value.
** Occupation included based on its highest interest area and third highest work value.
*** Occupation included based on its second highest interest area and highest work value.

ARTISTIC

ARTISTIC — ACHIEVEMENT

JOB ZONE 1 — ARTISTIC — ACHIEVEMENT

(No occupations for this combination in this job zone. To find occupations, look at other job zones in this combination or refer to the Interest and Work Value Master Lists.)

JOB ZONE 2 — ARTISTIC — ACHIEVEMENT

O*NET-SOC#	O*NET-SOC Title	O*NET-SOC#	O*NET-SOC Title
27-1023.00	Floral Designers	51-6041.00	Shoe and Leather Workers and Repairers***
39-5091.00	Makeup Artists, Theatrical and Performance	27-2042.01	Singers
27-3011.00	Radio and Television Announcers		

(To find more occupations, look at other job zones in this combination or refer to the Interest and Work Value Master Lists.)

JOB ZONE 3 — ARTISTIC — ACHIEVEMENT

O*NET-SOC#	O*NET-SOC Title	O*NET-SOC#	O*NET-SOC Title
27-2011.00	Actors	51-9131.01	Photographic Retouchers and Restorers
27-3043.03	Caption Writers	27-4021.01	Professional Photographers
51-9194.02	Engravers/Carvers***	27-3012.00	Public Address System and Other Announcers***
27-1022.00	Fashion Designers	27-1013.02	Sketch Artists
27-3091.00	Interpreters and Translators	27-4014.00	Sound Engineering Technicians***
27-1026.00	Merchandise Displayers and Window Trimmers	51-9195.03	Stone Cutters and Carvers***
25-4013.00	Museum Technicians and Conservators	49-9063.02	Stringed Instrument Repairers and Tuners***
27-4021.02	Photographers, Scientific		

---

* Occupation included based on its highest interest area and second highest work value.
** Occupation included based on its highest interest area and third highest work value.
*** Occupation included based on its second highest interest area and highest work value.

ARTISTIC — ACHIEVEMENT (continued)

JOB ZONE 4 — ARTISTIC — ACHIEVEMENT

O*NET-SOC#	O*NET-SOC Title	O*NET-SOC#	O*NET-SOC Title
25-3011.00	Adult Literacy, Remedial Education, and GED Teachers and Instructors***	27-1025.00	Interior Designers
11-2011.00	Advertising and Promotions Managers	25-2022.00	Middle School Teachers, Except Special and Vocational Education***
17-1011.00	Architects, Except Landscape and Naval	27-2041.02	Music Arrangers and Orchestrators
17-3011.01	Architectural Drafters***	27-1013.01	Painters and Illustrators
27-1011.00	Art Directors	51-5022.03	Photoengravers***
27-3021.00	Broadcast News Analysts	27-3043.01	Poets and Lyricists
27-4012.00	Broadcast Technicians***	27-3031.00	Public Relations Specialists***
27-4031.00	Camera Operators, Television, Video, and Motion Picture	27-3022.00	Reporters and Correspondents
		25-2031.00	Secondary School Teachers, Except Special and Vocational Education***
27-1013.03	Cartoonists		
27-1021.00	Commercial and Industrial Designers	25-3021.00	Self-Enrichment Education Teachers***
27-3043.02	Creative Writers	25-2042.00	Special Education Teachers, Middle School***
27-2031.00	Dancers	25-2041.00	Special Education Teachers, Preschool, Kindergarten, and Elementary School***
27-3041.00	Editors		
21-1012.00	Educational, Vocational, and School Counselors***	25-2043.00	Special Education Teachers, Secondary School***
25-2021.00	Elementary School Teachers, Except Special Education***	25-2023.00	Vocational Education Teachers, Middle School***
		25-2032.00	Vocational Education Teachers, Secondary School***
27-1027.02	Exhibit Designers		
27-1024.00	Graphic Designers		

JOB ZONE 5 — ARTISTIC — ACHIEVEMENT

O*NET-SOC#	O*NET-SOC Title	O*NET-SOC#	O*NET-SOC Title
25-1121.00	Art, Drama, and Music Teachers, Postsecondary	27-2041.01	Music Directors
21-2011.00	Clergy***	27-2042.02	Musicians, Instrumental
25-1123.00	English Language and Literature Teachers, Postsecondary	29-1066.00	Psychiatrists***
		27-1013.04	Sculptors
25-1124.00	Foreign Language and Literature Teachers, Postsecondary	27-1027.01	Set Designers
		27-3042.00	Technical Writers
17-1012.00	Landscape Architects		

---

* Occupation included based on its highest interest area and second highest work value.
** Occupation included based on its highest interest area and third highest work value.
*** Occupation included based on its second highest interest area and highest work value.

ARTISTIC — INDEPENDENCE

JOB ZONE 1 — ARTISTIC — INDEPENDENCE

(No occupations for this combination in this job zone. To find occupations, look at other job zones in this combination or refer to the Interest and Work Value Master Lists.)

JOB ZONE 2 — ARTISTIC — INDEPENDENCE

O*NET-SOC#	O*NET-SOC Title	O*NET-SOC#	O*NET-SOC Title
27-1023.00	Floral Designers*	27-3011.00	Radio and Television Announcers*
39-5091.00	Makeup Artists, Theatrical and Performance**	27-2042.01	Singers*

(To find more occupations, look at other job zones in this combination or refer to the Interest and Work Value Master Lists.)

JOB ZONE 3 — ARTISTIC — INDEPENDENCE

O*NET-SOC#	O*NET-SOC Title	O*NET-SOC#	O*NET-SOC Title
51-9194.03	Etchers***	27-2012.04	Talent Directors
19-3041.00	Sociologists***		

(To find more occupations, look at other job zones in this combination or refer to the Interest and Work Value Master Lists.)

JOB ZONE 4 — ARTISTIC — INDEPENDENCE

O*NET-SOC#	O*NET-SOC Title	O*NET-SOC#	O*NET-SOC Title
51-5022.04	Camera Operators***	27-4032.00	Film and Video Editors
19-3031.02	Clinical Psychologists***	19-3093.00	Historians***
27-3043.04	Copy Writers	25-2012.00	Kindergarten Teachers, Except Special Education***
39-3092.00	Costume Attendants		
25-4012.00	Curators	51-9195.05	Potters***
51-6052.02	Custom Tailors***	25-2011.00	Preschool Teachers, Except Special Education***
27-2012.02	Directors- Stage, Motion Pictures, Television, and Radio	27-2012.01	Producers
		27-2012.05	Technical Directors/Managers***

JOB ZONE 5 — ARTISTIC — INDEPENDENCE

O*NET-SOC#	O*NET-SOC Title	O*NET-SOC#	O*NET-SOC Title
27-2032.00	Choreographers	19-3094.00	Political Scientists***
27-2041.03	Composers	27-2012.03	Program Directors***

(To find more occupations, look at other job zones in this combination or refer to the Interest and Work Value Master Lists.)

* Occupation included based on its highest interest area and second highest work value.
** Occupation included based on its highest interest area and third highest work value.
*** Occupation included based on its second highest interest area and highest work value.

ARTISTIC — RECOGNITION

JOB ZONE 1 — ARTISTIC — RECOGNITION

(No occupations for this combination in this job zone. To find occupations, look at other job zones in this combination or refer to the Interest and Work Value Master Lists.)

JOB ZONE 2 — ARTISTIC — RECOGNITION

(No occupations for this combination in this job zone. To find occupations, look at other job zones in this combination or refer to the Interest and Work Value Master Lists.)

JOB ZONE 3 — ARTISTIC — RECOGNITION

O*NET-SOC#	*O*NET-SOC Title*
27-2012.04	Talent Directors**

(To find more occupations, look at other job zones in this combination or refer to the Interest and Work Value Master Lists.)

JOB ZONE 4 — ARTISTIC — RECOGNITION

O*NET-SOC#	*O*NET-SOC Title*	*O*NET-SOC#*	*O*NET-SOC Title*
27-1011.00	Art Directors**	27-2012.01	Producers**
27-2012.02	Directors- Stage, Motion Pictures, Television, and Radio**		

(To find more occupations, look at other job zones in this combination or refer to the Interest and Work Value Master Lists.)

JOB ZONE 5 — ARTISTIC — RECOGNITION

O*NET-SOC#	*O*NET-SOC Title*	*O*NET-SOC#*	*O*NET-SOC Title*
27-2032.00	Choreographers**	27-1027.01	Set Designers**
27-2041.01	Music Directors**		

(To find more occupations, look at other job zones in this combination or refer to the Interest and Work Value Master Lists.)

---

* Occupation included based on its highest interest area and second highest work value.
** Occupation included based on its highest interest area and third highest work value.
*** Occupation included based on its second highest interest area and highest work value.

ARTISTIC — RELATIONSHIPS

JOB ZONE 1 — ARTISTIC — RELATIONSHIPS

O*NET-SOC#	O*NET-SOC Title
39-9011.00	Child Care Workers***

(To find more occupations, look at other job zones in this combination or refer to the Interest and Work Value Master Lists.)

JOB ZONE 2 — ARTISTIC — RELATIONSHIPS

O*NET-SOC#	O*NET-SOC Title
39-5091.00	Makeup Artists, Theatrical and Performance

(To find more occupations, look at other job zones in this combination or refer to the Interest and Work Value Master Lists.)

JOB ZONE 3 — ARTISTIC — RELATIONSHIPS

O*NET-SOC#	O*NET-SOC Title
51-3011.01	Bakers, Bread and Pastry***
39-9032.00	Recreation Workers***

(To find more occupations, look at other job zones in this combination or refer to the Interest and Work Value Master Lists.)

JOB ZONE 4 — ARTISTIC — RELATIONSHIPS

O*NET-SOC#	O*NET-SOC Title
25-4021.00	Librarians
29-1125.00	Recreational Therapists***

(To find more occupations, look at other job zones in this combination or refer to the Interest and Work Value Master Lists.)

JOB ZONE 5 — ARTISTIC — RELATIONSHIPS

O*NET-SOC#	O*NET-SOC Title	O*NET-SOC#	O*NET-SOC Title
25-1121.00	Art, Drama, and Music Teachers, Postsecondary**	25-1124.00	Foreign Language and Literature Teachers, Postsecondary**
25-1123.00	English Language and Literature Teachers, Postsecondary**		

(To find more occupations, look at other job zones in this combination or refer to the Interest and Work Value Master Lists.)

---

* Occupation included based on its highest interest area and second highest work value.
** Occupation included based on its highest interest area and third highest work value.
*** Occupation included based on its second highest interest area and highest work value.

ARTISTIC

ARTISTIC — SUPPORT

JOB ZONE 1 — ARTISTIC — SUPPORT

O*NET-SOC#	O*NET-SOC Title
51-9194.05	Etchers, Hand***

(To find more occupations, look at other job zones in this combination or refer to the Interest and Work Value Master Lists.)

JOB ZONE 2 — ARTISTIC — SUPPORT

(No occupations for this combination in this job zone. To find occupations, look at other job zones in this combination or refer to the Interest and Work Value Master Lists.)

JOB ZONE 3 — ARTISTIC — SUPPORT

O*NET-SOC#	O*NET-SOC Title
51-9194.06	Engravers,Hand***
51-3011.01	Bakers, Bread and Pastry***

(To find more occupations, look at other job zones in this combination or refer to the Interest and Work Value Master Lists.)

JOB ZONE 4 — ARTISTIC — SUPPORT

O*NET-SOC#	O*NET-SOC Title
51-5012.00	Bookbinders***

(To find more occupations, look at other job zones in this combination or refer to the Interest and Work Value Master Lists.)

JOB ZONE 5 — ARTISTIC — SUPPORT

(No occupations for this combination in this job zone. To find occupations, look at other job zones in this combination or refer to the Interest and Work Value Master Lists.)

---

* Occupation included based on its highest interest area and second highest work value.
** Occupation included based on its highest interest area and third highest work value.
*** Occupation included based on its second highest interest area and highest work value.

ARTISTIC — WORKING CONDITIONS

JOB ZONE 1 — ARTISTIC — WORKING CONDITIONS

O*NET-SOC#	O*NET-SOC Title
41-9012.00	Models

(To find more occupations, look at other job zones in this combination or refer to the Interest and Work Value Master Lists.)

JOB ZONE 2 — ARTISTIC — WORKING CONDITIONS

O*NET-SOC#	O*NET-SOC Title
51-9131.03	Photographic Hand Developers***

(To find more occupations, look at other job zones in this combination or refer to the Interest and Work Value Master Lists.)

JOB ZONE 3 — ARTISTIC — WORKING CONDITIONS

O*NET-SOC#	O*NET-SOC Title	O*NET-SOC#	O*NET-SOC Title
49-9063.01	Keyboard Instrument Repairers and Tuners***	49-9063.02	Stringed Instrument Repairers and Tuners***
49-9063.04	Percussion Instrument Repairers and Tuners***		

(To find more occupations, look at other job zones in this combination or refer to the Interest and Work Value Master Lists.)

JOB ZONE 4 — ARTISTIC — WORKING CONDITIONS

O*NET-SOC#	O*NET-SOC Title
43-9031.00	Desktop Publishers***
49-9063.03	Reed or Wind Instrument Repairers and Tuners***

(To find more occupations, look at other job zones in this combination or refer to the Interest and Work Value Master Lists.)

JOB ZONE 5 — ARTISTIC — WORKING CONDITIONS

(No occupations for this combination in this job zone. To find occupations, look at other job zones in this combination or refer to the Interest and Work Value Master Lists.)

---

* Occupation included based on its highest interest area and second highest work value.
** Occupation included based on its highest interest area and third highest work value.
*** Occupation included based on its second highest interest area and highest work value.

SOCIAL

SOCIAL — ACHIEVEMENT

JOB ZONE 1 — SOCIAL — ACHIEVEMENT

O*NET-SOC#	O*NET-SOC Title
53-3011.00	Ambulance Drivers and Attendants, Except Emergency Medical Technicians**

(To find more occupations, look at other job zones in this combination or refer to the Interest and Work Value Master Lists.)

JOB ZONE 2 — SOCIAL — ACHIEVEMENT

O*NET-SOC#	O*NET-SOC Title	O*NET-SOC#	O*NET-SOC Title
29-2041.00	Emergency Medical Technicians and Paramedics	41-4012.00	Sales Representatives, Wholesale and Manufacturing, Except Technical and Scientific Products***
33-2011.02	Forest Fire Fighters***		
33-2011.01	Municipal Fire Fighters***		
33-9021.00	Private Detectives and Investigators***	33-3051.03	Sheriffs and Deputy Sheriffs
27-3011.00	Radio and Television Announcers***	33-3052.00	Transit and Railroad Police***

JOB ZONE 3 — SOCIAL — ACHIEVEMENT

O*NET-SOC#	O*NET-SOC Title	O*NET-SOC#	O*NET-SOC Title
41-3011.00	Advertising Sales Agents***	33-3051.01	Police Patrol Officers
27-3043.03	Caption Writers***	27-3012.00	Public Address System and Other Announcers
41-3021.00	Insurance Sales Agents***	41-4011.02	Sales Representatives, Chemical and Pharmaceutical***
27-3091.00	Interpreters and Translators***		
29-2091.00	Orthotists and Prosthetists	27-2023.00	Umpires, Referees, and Other Sports Officials***

---

* Occupation included based on its highest interest area and second highest work value.
** Occupation included based on its highest interest area and third highest work value.
*** Occupation included based on its second highest interest area and highest work value.

SOCIAL — ACHIEVEMENT (continued)

JOB ZONE 4 — SOCIAL — ACHIEVEMENT

O*NET-SOC#	O*NET-SOC Title	O*NET-SOC#	O*NET-SOC Title
25-3011.00	Adult Literacy, Remedial Education, and GED Teachers and Instructors	29-1122.00	Occupational Therapists
		29-1123.00	Physical Therapists
29-1121.00	Audiologists	29-1081.00	Podiatrists
21-1021.00	Child, Family, and School Social Workers	29-1111.00	Registered Nurses
11-9032.00	Education Administrators, Elementary and Secondary School	25-2031.00	Secondary School Teachers, Except Special and Vocational Education
11-9031.00	Education Administrators, Preschool and Child Care Center/Program	25-3021.00	Self-Enrichment Education Teachers
		11-9151.00	Social and Community Service Managers
21-1012.00	Educational, Vocational, and School Counselors	25-2042.00	Special Education Teachers, Middle School
25-2021.00	Elementary School Teachers, Except Special Education	25-2041.00	Special Education Teachers, Preschool, Kindergarten, and Elementary School
25-9021.00	Farm and Home Management Advisors	25-2043.00	Special Education Teachers, Secondary School
21-1022.00	Medical and Public Health Social Workers	29-1127.00	Speech-Language Pathologists
21-1023.00	Mental Health and Substance Abuse Social Workers	21-1011.00	Substance Abuse and Behavioral Disorder Counselors
21-1014.00	Mental Health Counselors	25-1194.00	Vocational Education Teachers, Postsecondary
25-2022.00	Middle School Teachers, Except Special and Vocational Education	25-2023.00	Vocational Education Teachers, Middle School
		25-2032.00	Vocational Education Teachers, Secondary School

JOB ZONE 5 — SOCIAL — ACHIEVEMENT

O*NET-SOC#	O*NET-SOC Title	O*NET-SOC#	O*NET-SOC Title
25-1041.00	Agricultural Sciences Teachers, Postsecondary***	25-1124.00	Foreign Language and Literature Teachers, Postsecondary***
25-1061.00	Anthropology and Archeology Teachers, Postsecondary	25-1043.00	Forestry and Conservation Science Teachers, Postsecondary***
25-1062.00	Area, Ethnic, and Cultural Studies Teachers, Postsecondary	21-1091.00	Health Educators
25-1121.00	Art, Drama, and Music Teachers, Postsecondary***	25-1071.00	Health Specialties Teachers, Postsecondary***
29-9091.00	Athletic Trainers	25-1125.00	History Teachers, Postsecondary
25-1042.00	Biological Science Teachers, Postsecondary***	25-1022.00	Mathematical Science Teachers, Postsecondary***
25-1052.00	Chemistry Teachers, Postsecondary***	27-2041.01	Music Directors***
21-2011.00	Clergy	25-1072.00	Nursing Instructors and Teachers, Postsecondary
19-3031.03	Counseling Psychologists	25-1054.00	Physics Teachers, Postsecondary***
21-2021.00	Directors, Religious Activities and Education	25-1065.00	Political Science Teachers, Postsecondary
25-1063.00	Economics Teachers, Postsecondary	25-1066.00	Psychology Teachers, Postsecondary
11-9033.00	Education Administrators, Postsecondary***	25-1067.00	Sociology Teachers, Postsecondary
25-1123.00	English Language and Literature Teachers, Postsecondary***		

---

* Occupation included based on its highest interest area and second highest work value.
** Occupation included based on its highest interest area and third highest work value.
*** Occupation included based on its second highest interest area and highest work value.

SOCIAL — INDEPENDENCE

JOB ZONE 1 — SOCIAL — INDEPENDENCE

(No occupations for this combination in this job zone. To find occupations, look at other job zones in this combination or refer to the Interest and Work Value Master Lists.)

JOB ZONE 2 — SOCIAL — INDEPENDENCE

O*NET-SOC#	O*NET-SOC Title
41-9022.00	Real Estate Sales Agents***
41-4012.00	Sales Representatives, Wholesale and Manufacturing, Except Technical and Scientific Products***

(To find more occupations, look at other job zones in this combination or refer to the Interest and Work Value Master Lists.)

JOB ZONE 3 — SOCIAL — INDEPENDENCE

O*NET-SOC#	O*NET-SOC Title	O*NET-SOC#	O*NET-SOC Title
13-1011.00	Agents and Business Managers of Artists, Performers, and Athletes***	43-1011.01	First-Line Supervisors, Customer Service***
		39-9031.00	Fitness Trainers and Aerobics Instructors
39-2011.00	Animal Trainers	41-4011.05	Sales Representatives, Medical***

(To find more occupations, look at other job zones in this combination or refer to the Interest and Work Value Master Lists.)

JOB ZONE 4 — SOCIAL — INDEPENDENCE

O*NET-SOC#	O*NET-SOC Title	O*NET-SOC#	O*NET-SOC Title
19-3091.01	Anthropologists***	19-1031.03	Park Naturalists
11-9061.00	Funeral Directors***	25-2011.00	Preschool Teachers, Except Special Education
25-2012.00	Kindergarten Teachers, Except Special Education	13-1073.00	Training and Development Specialists
11-9111.00	Medical and Health Services Managers***		

JOB ZONE 5 — SOCIAL — INDEPENDENCE

O*NET-SOC#	O*NET-SOC Title	O*NET-SOC#	O*NET-SOC Title
23-1021.00	Administrative Law Judges, Adjudicators, and Hearing Officers***	25-9031.00	Instructional Coordinators
		23-1023.00	Judges, Magistrate Judges, and Magistrates***
23-1022.00	Arbitrators, Mediators, and Conciliators***	29-9011.00	Occupational Health and Safety Specialists
27-2032.00	Choreographers***		

---

* Occupation included based on its highest interest area and second highest work value.
** Occupation included based on its highest interest area and third highest work value.
*** Occupation included based on its second highest interest area and highest work value.

SOCIAL — RECOGNITION

JOB ZONE 1 — SOCIAL — RECOGNITION

(No occupations for this combination in this job zone. To find occupations, look at other job zones in this combination or refer to the Interest and Work Value Master Lists.)

JOB ZONE 2 — SOCIAL — RECOGNITION

*O*NET-SOC#* *O*NET-SOC Title*
43-5031.00   Police, Fire, and Ambulance Dispatchers**

(To find more occupations, look at other job zones in this combination or refer to the Interest and Work Value Master Lists.)

JOB ZONE 3 — SOCIAL — RECOGNITION

(No occupations for this combination in this job zone. To find occupations, look at other job zones in this combination or refer to the Interest and Work Value Master Lists.)

JOB ZONE 4 — SOCIAL — RECOGNITION

*O*NET-SOC#*	*O*NET-SOC Title*	*O*NET-SOC#*	*O*NET-SOC Title*
11-9032.00	Education Administrators, Elementary and Secondary School*	11-9031.00	Education Administrators, Preschool and Child Care Center/Program*

(To find more occupations, look at other job zones in this combination or refer to the Interest and Work Value Master Lists.)

JOB ZONE 5 — SOCIAL — RECOGNITION

*O*NET-SOC#* *O*NET-SOC Title*
21-2011.00   Clergy**
25-9031.00   Instructional Coordinators**

(To find more occupations, look at other job zones in this combination or refer to the Interest and Work Value Master Lists.)

---

* Occupation included based on its highest interest area and second highest work value.
** Occupation included based on its highest interest area and third highest work value.
*** Occupation included based on its second highest interest area and highest work value.

SOCIAL — RELATIONSHIPS

JOB ZONE 1 — SOCIAL — RELATIONSHIPS

O*NET-SOC#	O*NET-SOC Title	O*NET-SOC#	O*NET-SOC Title
53-3011.00	Ambulance Drivers and Attendants, Except Emergency Medical Technicians	31-1011.00	Home Health Aides
35-3011.00	Bartenders***	39-3093.00	Locker Room, Coatroom, and Dressing Room Attendants
39-9011.00	Child Care Workers	39-5092.00	Manicurists and Pedicurists***
35-3022.00	Counter Attendants, Cafeteria, Food Concession, and Coffee Shop	39-6021.00	Tour Guides and Escorts
33-9091.00	Crossing Guards	39-6032.00	Transportation Attendants, Except Flight Attendants and Baggage Porters***
35-3041.00	Food Servers, Nonrestaurant	39-3031.00	Ushers, Lobby Attendants, and Ticket Takers
39-4021.00	Funeral Attendants	35-3031.00	Waiters and Waitresses

JOB ZONE 2 — SOCIAL — RELATIONSHIPS

O*NET-SOC#	O*NET-SOC Title	O*NET-SOC#	O*NET-SOC Title
39-6031.00	Flight Attendants***	31-2022.00	Physical Therapist Aides
25-4031.00	Library Technicians***	31-2021.00	Physical Therapist Assistants
33-9092.00	Lifeguards, Ski Patrol, and Other Recreational Protective Service Workers***	31-1013.00	Psychiatric Aides
		21-1093.00	Social and Human Service Assistants
31-1012.00	Nursing Aides, Orderlies, and Attendants	41-3041.00	Travel Agents***
31-2012.00	Occupational Therapist Aides	43-4181.01	Travel Clerks***
31-2011.00	Occupational Therapist Assistants	39-6022.00	Travel Guides***
39-9021.00	Personal and Home Care Aides	43-4061.02	Welfare Eligibility Workers and Interviewers

JOB ZONE 3 — SOCIAL — RELATIONSHIPS

O*NET-SOC#	O*NET-SOC Title	O*NET-SOC#	O*NET-SOC Title
39-5011.00	Barbers***	29-2061.00	Licensed Practical and Licensed Vocational Nurses
31-9091.00	Dental Assistants	31-9092.00	Medical Assistants
29-2021.00	Dental Hygienists	13-2052.00	Personal Financial Advisors
13-1071.01	Employment Interviewers, Private or Public Employment Service	29-2053.00	Psychiatric Technicians
		39-9032.00	Recreation Workers
39-5012.00	Hairdressers, Hairstylists, and Cosmetologists***	39-9041.00	Residential Advisors
35-9031.00	Hosts and Hostesses, Restaurant, Lounge, and Coffee Shop***	29-2055.00	Surgical Technologists***
		25-9041.00	Teacher Assistants

* Occupation included based on its highest interest area and second highest work value.
** Occupation included based on its highest interest area and third highest work value.
*** Occupation included based on its second highest interest area and highest work value.

SOCIAL — RELATIONSHIPS (continued)

JOB ZONE 4 — SOCIAL — RELATIONSHIPS

O*NET-SOC#	O*NET-SOC Title	O*NET-SOC#	O*NET-SOC Title
27-4011.00	Audio and Video Equipment Technicians***	29-1123.00	Physical Therapists*
29-1121.00	Audiologists*	29-1124.00	Radiation Therapists
25-9011.00	Audio-Visual Collections Specialists***	29-1125.00	Recreational Therapists
29-2051.00	Dietetic Technicians	29-1111.00	Registered Nurses*
29-1122.00	Occupational Therapists*	29-1127.00	Speech-Language Pathologists*

JOB ZONE 5 — SOCIAL — RELATIONSHIPS

O*NET-SOC#	O*NET-SOC Title	O*NET-SOC#	O*NET-SOC Title
25-1061.00	Anthropology and Archeology Teachers, Postsecondary**	21-1091.00	Health Educators*
25-1062.00	Area, Ethnic, and Cultural Studies Teachers, Postsecondary**	25-1125.00	History Teachers, Postsecondary**
		25-1072.00	Nursing Instructors and Teachers, Postsecondary**
29-9091.00	Athletic Trainers	25-1065.00	Political Science Teachers, Postsecondary**
25-1063.00	Economics Teachers, Postsecondary**	25-1066.00	Psychology Teachers, Postsecondary**
25-1191.00	Graduate Teaching Assistants	25-1067.00	Sociology Teachers, Postsecondary**

* Occupation included based on its highest interest area and second highest work value.
** Occupation included based on its highest interest area and third highest work value.
*** Occupation included based on its second highest interest area and highest work value.

SOCIAL — SUPPORT

JOB ZONE 1 — SOCIAL — SUPPORT

O*NET-SOC#	O*NET-SOC Title	O*NET-SOC#	O*NET-SOC Title
33-3011.00	Bailiffs	33-9032.00	Security Guards
53-3021.00	Bus Drivers, Transit and Intercity***		

(To find more occupations, look at other job zones in this combination or refer to the Interest and Work Value Master Lists.)

JOB ZONE 2 — SOCIAL — SUPPORT

O*NET-SOC#	O*NET-SOC Title	O*NET-SOC#	O*NET-SOC Title
33-9011.00	Animal Control Workers	43-5031.00	Police, Fire, and Ambulance Dispatchers
53-3022.00	Bus Drivers, School***	41-2031.00	Retail Salespersons***
43-4061.01	Claims Takers, Unemployment Benefits***	21-1093.00	Social and Human Service Assistants
33-3012.00	Correctional Officers and Jailers***	43-4181.01	Travel Clerks***

JOB ZONE 3 — SOCIAL — SUPPORT

O*NET-SOC#	O*NET-SOC Title
13-1071.02	Personnel Recruiters***
21-1092.00	Probation Officers and Correctional Treatment Specialists

(To find more occupations, look at other job zones in this combination or refer to the Interest and Work Value Master Lists.)

JOB ZONE 4 — SOCIAL — SUPPORT

O*NET-SOC#	O*NET-SOC Title	O*NET-SOC#	O*NET-SOC Title
13-1041.03	Equal Opportunity Representatives and Officers	13-2072.00	Loan Officers***
13-2071.00	Loan Counselors***		

(To find more occupations, look at other job zones in this combination or refer to the Interest and Work Value Master Lists.)

JOB ZONE 5 — SOCIAL — SUPPORT

O*NET-SOC#	O*NET-SOC Title
25-1191.00	Graduate Teaching Assistants**

(To find more occupations, look at other job zones in this combination or refer to the Interest and Work Value Master Lists.)

---

* Occupation included based on its highest interest area and second highest work value.
** Occupation included based on its highest interest area and third highest work value.
*** Occupation included based on its second highest interest area and highest work value.

SOCIAL — WORKING CONDITIONS

JOB ZONE 1 — SOCIAL — WORKING CONDITIONS

O*NET-SOC#	O*NET-SOC Title
39-9011.00	Child Care Workers*

(To find more occupations, look at other job zones in this combination or refer to the Interest and Work Value Master Lists.)

JOB ZONE 2 — SOCIAL — WORKING CONDITIONS

(No occupations for this combination in this job zone. To find occupations, look at other job zones in this combination or refer to the Interest and Work Value Master Lists.)

JOB ZONE 3 — SOCIAL — WORKING CONDITIONS

(No occupations for this combination in this job zone. To find occupations, look at other job zones in this combination or refer to the Interest and Work Value Master Lists.)

JOB ZONE 4 — SOCIAL — WORKING CONDITIONS

(No occupations for this combination in this job zone. To find occupations, look at other job zones in this combination or refer to the Interest and Work Value Master Lists.)

JOB ZONE 5 — SOCIAL — WORKING CONDITIONS

O*NET-SOC#	O*NET-SOC Title
19-3031.03	Counseling Psychologists**

(To find more occupations, look at other job zones in this combination or refer to the Interest and Work Value Master Lists.)

---

* Occupation included based on its highest interest area and second highest work value.
** Occupation included based on its highest interest area and third highest work value.
*** Occupation included based on its second highest interest area and highest work value.

ENTERPRISING

ENTERPRISING — ACHIEVEMENT

JOB ZONE 1 — ENTERPRISING — ACHIEVEMENT

(No occupations for this combination in this job zone. To find occupations, look at other job zones in this combination or refer to the Interest and Work Value Master Lists.)

JOB ZONE 2 — ENTERPRISING — ACHIEVEMENT

O*NET-SOC#	O*NET-SOC Title	O*NET-SOC#	O*NET-SOC Title
33-9021.00	Private Detectives and Investigators	41-4012.00	Sales Representatives, Wholesale and Manufacturing, Except Technical and Scientific Products
41-4011.01	Sales Representatives, Agricultural		
41-4011.03	Sales Representatives, Electrical/Electronic		
41-4011.04	Sales Representatives, Mechanical Equipment and Supplies	33-3051.03	Sheriffs and Deputy Sheriffs***
		27-2042.01	Singers***
		33-3052.00	Transit and Railroad Police

JOB ZONE 3 — ENTERPRISING — ACHIEVEMENT

O*NET-SOC#	O*NET-SOC Title	O*NET-SOC#	O*NET-SOC Title
27-2011.00	Actors***	33-3051.02	Highway Patrol Pilots***
41-3011.00	Advertising Sales Agents	13-1031.02	Insurance Adjusters, Examiners, and Investigators
27-2021.00	Athletes and Sports Competitors	41-3021.00	Insurance Sales Agents
27-1022.00	Fashion Designers***	41-4011.02	Sales Representatives, Chemical and Pharmaceutical
39-1021.00	First-Line Supervisors/Managers of Personal Service Workers	27-2023.00	Umpires, Referees, and Other Sports Officials

* Occupation included based on its highest interest area and second highest work value.
** Occupation included based on its highest interest area and third highest work value.
*** Occupation included based on its second highest interest area and highest work value.

ENTERPRISING — ACHIEVEMENT (continued)

JOB ZONE 4 — ENTERPRISING — ACHIEVEMENT

O*NET-SOC#	O*NET-SOC Title	O*NET-SOC#	O*NET-SOC Title
11-2011.00	Advertising and Promotions Managers***	27-1024.00	Graphic Designers***
53-2011.00	Airline Pilots, Copilots, and Flight Engineers***	11-3040.00	Human Resources Managers
27-1011.00	Art Directors***	27-1025.00	Interior Designers***
27-1013.03	Cartoonists***	51-9071.01	Jewelers***
33-3021.04	Child Support, Missing Persons, and Unemployment Insurance Fraud Investigators	13-1111.00	Management Analysts
		19-3021.00	Market Research Analysts***
53-2012.00	Commercial Pilots***	11-2021.00	Marketing Managers
11-3041.00	Compensation and Benefits Managers	33-1021.01	Municipal Fire Fighting and Prevention Supervisors***
33-3021.03	Criminal Investigators and Special Agents		
29-1031.00	Dietitians and Nutritionists***	29-2081.00	Opticians, Dispensing
11-9032.00	Education Administrators, Elementary and Secondary School***	33-3021.01	Police Detectives
		27-3031.00	Public Relations Specialists
11-9031.00	Education Administrators, Preschool and Child Care Center/Program***	13-1023.00	Purchasing Agents, Except Wholesale, Retail, and Farm Products
11-3031.02	Financial Managers, Branch or Department	11-9151.00	Social and Community Service Managers***
33-1012.00	First-Line Supervisors/Managers of Police and Detectives	17-1022.00	Surveyors***
		11-3042.00	Training and Development Managers
11-1011.01	Government Service Executives	19-3051.00	Urban and Regional Planners***

JOB ZONE 5 — ENTERPRISING — ACHIEVEMENT

O*NET-SOC#	O*NET-SOC Title	O*NET-SOC#	O*NET-SOC Title
21-2021.00	Directors, Religious Activities and Education***	23-1011.00	Lawyers
19-3011.00	Economists***	41-9031.00	Sales Engineers
11-9033.00	Education Administrators, Postsecondary	53-5031.00	Ship Engineers***
21-1091.00	Health Educators***	11-3031.01	Treasurers, Controllers, and Chief Financial Officers

* Occupation included based on its highest interest area and second highest work value.
** Occupation included based on its highest interest area and third highest work value.
*** Occupation included based on its second highest interest area and highest work value.

ENTERPRISING — INDEPENDENCE

JOB ZONE 1 — ENTERPRISING — INDEPENDENCE

(No occupations for this combination in this job zone. To find occupations, look at other job zones in this combination or refer to the Interest and Work Value Master Lists.)

JOB ZONE 2 — ENTERPRISING — INDEPENDENCE

O*NET-SOC#	O*NET-SOC Title	O*NET-SOC#	O*NET-SOC Title
53-5022.00	Motorboat Operators***	41-4012.00	Sales Representatives, Wholesale and Manufacturing, Except Technical and Scientific Products
33-9021.00	Private Detectives and Investigators*		
41-9022.00	Real Estate Sales Agents	33-3052.00	Transit and Railroad Police*
41-4011.01	Sales Representatives, Agricultural*	41-3041.00	Travel Agents*
41-4011.03	Sales Representatives, Electrical/Electronic*	39-6022.00	Travel Guides*
41-4011.04	Sales Representatives, Mechanical Equipment and Supplies*		

JOB ZONE 3 — ENTERPRISING — INDEPENDENCE

O*NET-SOC#	O*NET-SOC Title	O*NET-SOC#	O*NET-SOC Title
13-1011.00	Agents and Business Managers of Artists, Performers, and Athletes	51-1011.00	First-Line Supervisors/Managers of Production and Operating Workers
47-1011.02	First-Line Supervisors and Manager/Supervisors-Extractive Workers	41-1011.00	First-Line Supervisors/Managers of Retail Sales Workers
45-1011.01	First-Line Supervisors and Manager/Supervisors - Agricultural Crop Workers	53-1031.00	First-Line Supervisors/Managers of Transportation and Material-Moving Machine and Vehicle Operators
45-1011.02	First-Line Supervisors and Manager/Supervisors - Animal Husbandry Workers	11-9071.00	Gaming Managers
43-1011.02	First-Line Supervisors, Administrative Support	39-1011.00	Gaming Supervisors
43-1011.01	First-Line Supervisors, Customer Service	37-1011.02	Janitorial Supervisors
35-1012.00	First-Line Supervisors/Managers of Food Preparation and Serving Workers	11-9081.00	Lodging Managers
		41-3031.02	Sales Agents, Financial Services
53-1021.00	First-Line Supervisors/Managers of Helpers, Laborers, and Material Movers, Hand	41-4011.06	Sales Representatives, Instruments
		41-4011.05	Sales Representatives, Medical
41-1012.00	First-Line Supervisors/Managers of Non-Retail Sales Workers	13-1022.00	Wholesale and Retail Buyers, Except Farm Products
39-1021.00	First-Line Supervisors/Managers of Personal Service Workers		

* Occupation included based on its highest interest area and second highest work value.
** Occupation included based on its highest interest area and third highest work value.
*** Occupation included based on its second highest interest area and highest work value.

ENTERPRISING — INDEPENDENCE (continued)

JOB ZONE 4 — ENTERPRISING — INDEPENDENCE

O*NET-SOC#	O*NET-SOC Title	O*NET-SOC#	O*NET-SOC Title
11-3011.00	Administrative Services Managers	11-3051.00	Industrial Production Managers
11-9011.02	Agricultural Crop Farm Managers	37-1012.01	Lawn Service Managers
13-2021.02	Appraisers, Real Estate	11-9111.00	Medical and Health Services Managers
35-1011.00	Chefs and Head Cooks	13-1121.00	Meeting and Convention Planners
11-9021.00	Construction Managers	11-9011.01	Nursery and Greenhouse Managers
47-1011.01	First-Line Supervisors and Manager/Supervisors- Construction Trades Workers	11-9141.00	Property, Real Estate, and Community Association Managers
49-1011.00	First-Line Supervisors/Managers of Mechanics, Installers, and Repairers	13-1021.00	Purchasing Agents and Buyers, Farm Products
		41-3031.01	Sales Agents, Securities and Commodities
11-9011.03	Fish Hatchery Managers	11-2022.00	Sales Managers
11-9051.00	Food Service Managers	53-5021.01	Ship and Boat Captains
11-9061.00	Funeral Directors	11-3071.02	Storage and Distribution Managers
11-1011.01	Government Service Executives	11-3071.01	Transportation Managers
17-2112.00	Industrial Engineers		

JOB ZONE 5 — ENTERPRISING — INDEPENDENCE

O*NET-SOC#	O*NET-SOC Title	O*NET-SOC#	O*NET-SOC Title
23-1021.00	Administrative Law Judges, Adjudicators, and Hearing Officers	19-3032.00	Industrial-Organizational Psychologists***
		23-1023.00	Judges, Magistrate Judges, and Magistrates
23-1022.00	Arbitrators, Mediators, and Conciliators	11-9121.00	Natural Sciences Managers***
27-2022.00	Coaches and Scouts	29-9011.00	Occupational Health and Safety Specialists***
11-3021.00	Computer and Information Systems Managers	53-5021.03	Pilots, Ship***
11-9041.00	Engineering Managers	11-1011.02	Private Sector Executives
33-1021.02	Forest Fire Fighting and Prevention Supervisors***	27-2012.03	Program Directors

* Occupation included based on its highest interest area and second highest work value.
** Occupation included based on its highest interest area and third highest work value.
*** Occupation included based on its second highest interest area and highest work value.

ENTERPRISING — RECOGNITION

JOB ZONE 1 — ENTERPRISING — RECOGNITION

(No occupations for this combination in this job zone. To find occupations, look at other job zones in this combination or refer to the Interest and Work Value Master Lists.)

JOB ZONE 2 — ENTERPRISING — RECOGNITION

O*NET-SOC#	O*NET-SOC Title
41-9022.00	Real Estate Sales Agents**

(To find more occupations, look at other job zones in this combination or refer to the Interest and Work Value Master Lists.)

JOB ZONE 3 — ENTERPRISING — RECOGNITION

O*NET-SOC#	O*NET-SOC Title	O*NET-SOC#	O*NET-SOC Title
27-2021.00	Athletes and Sports Competitors**	41-1012.00	First-Line Supervisors/Managers of Non-Retail Sales Workers*
45-1011.01	First-Line Supervisors and Manager/Supervisors - Agricultural Crop Workers**	51-1011.00	First-Line Supervisors/Managers of Production and Operating Workers**
45-1011.02	First-Line Supervisors and Manager/Supervisors - Animal Husbandry Workers**	41-1011.00	First-Line Supervisors/Managers of Retail Sales Workers*
47-1011.02	First-Line Supervisors and Manager/Supervisors-Extractive Workers**	53-1031.00	First-Line Supervisors/Managers of Transportation and Material-Moving Machine and Vehicle Operators**
43-1011.02	First-Line Supervisors, Administrative Support**	27-2023.00	Umpires, Referees, and Other Sports Officials**
43-1011.01	First-Line Supervisors, Customer Service**		
53-1021.00	First-Line Supervisors/Managers of Helpers, Laborers, and Material Movers, Hand*		

JOB ZONE 4 — ENTERPRISING — RECOGNITION

O*NET-SOC#	O*NET-SOC Title	O*NET-SOC#	O*NET-SOC Title
11-3011.00	Administrative Services Managers*	33-1012.00	First-Line Supervisors/Managers of Police and Detectives**
13-2061.00	Financial Examiners*	17-2112.00	Industrial Engineers**
11-3031.02	Financial Managers, Branch or Department*	41-3031.01	Sales Agents, Securities and Commodities**
47-1011.01	First-Line Supervisors and Manager/Supervisors-Construction Trades Workers*	11-2022.00	Sales Managers*
49-1011.00	First-Line Supervisors/Managers of Mechanics, Installers, and Repairers*	53-5021.01	Ship and Boat Captains**

JOB ZONE 5 — ENTERPRISING — RECOGNITION

O*NET-SOC#	O*NET-SOC Title	O*NET-SOC#	O*NET-SOC Title
27-2022.00	Coaches and Scouts**	11-3031.01	Treasurers, Controllers, and Chief Financial Officers**
11-9033.00	Education Administrators, Postsecondary*		
27-2012.03	Program Directors**		

(To find more occupations, look at other job zones in this combination or refer to the Interest and Work Value Master Lists.)

* Occupation included based on its highest interest area and second highest work value.
** Occupation included based on its highest interest area and third highest work value.
*** Occupation included based on its second highest interest area and highest work value.

ENTERPRISING — RELATIONSHIPS

JOB ZONE 1 — ENTERPRISING — RELATIONSHIPS

O*NET-SOC#	O*NET-SOC Title	O*NET-SOC#	O*NET-SOC Title
39-6011.00	Baggage Porters and Bellhops	39-5092.00	Manicurists and Pedicurists
35-3011.00	Bartenders	53-6021.00	Parking Lot Attendants***
35-2015.00	Cooks, Short Order***	53-6031.00	Service Station Attendants***
41-2021.00	Counter and Rental Clerks***	53-3041.00	Taxi Drivers and Chauffeurs***
41-9011.00	Demonstrators and Product Promoters	39-6021.00	Tour Guides and Escorts***
35-9011.00	Dining Room and Cafeteria Attendants and Bartender Helpers***	39-6032.00	Transportation Attendants, Except Flight Attendants and Baggage Porters
39-4021.00	Funeral Attendants***	35-3031.00	Waiters and Waitresses***
39-3093.00	Locker Room, Coatroom, and Dressing Room Attendants***		

JOB ZONE 2 — ENTERPRISING — RELATIONSHIPS

O*NET-SOC#	O*NET-SOC Title	O*NET-SOC#	O*NET-SOC Title
39-6031.00	Flight Attendants	41-3041.00	Travel Agents
43-4081.00	Hotel, Motel, and Resort Desk Clerks***	39-6022.00	Travel Guides
43-3071.00	Tellers***		

JOB ZONE 3 — ENTERPRISING — RELATIONSHIPS

O*NET-SOC#	O*NET-SOC Title	O*NET-SOC#	O*NET-SOC Title
51-3021.00	Butchers and Meat Cutters***	39-5012.00	Hairdressers, Hairstylists, and Cosmetologists
35-2014.00	Cooks, Restaurant***	35-9031.00	Hosts and Hostesses, Restaurant, Lounge, and Coffee Shop
13-1071.01	Employment Interviewers, Private or Public Employment Service***	13-2052.00	Personal Financial Advisors***

JOB ZONE 4 — ENTERPRISING — RELATIONSHIPS

O*NET-SOC#	O*NET-SOC Title
37-1011.01	Housekeeping Supervisors
29-2081.00	Opticians, Dispensing*

(To find more occupations, look at other job zones in this combination or refer to the Interest and Work Value Master Lists.)

JOB ZONE 5 — ENTERPRISING — RELATIONSHIPS

(No occupations for this combination in this job zone. To find occupations, look at other job zones in this combination or refer to the Interest and Work Value Master Lists.)

---

* Occupation included based on its highest interest area and second highest work value.
** Occupation included based on its highest interest area and third highest work value.
*** Occupation included based on its second highest interest area and highest work value.

ENTERPRISING — SUPPORT

JOB ZONE 1 — ENTERPRISING — SUPPORT

O*NET-SOC#	O*NET-SOC Title	O*NET-SOC#	O*NET-SOC Title
33-3011.00	Bailiffs***	43-4071.00	File Clerks***
41-2011.00	Cashiers***	43-3061.00	Procurement Clerks***
43-4041.01	Credit Authorizers***	43-4171.00	Receptionists and Information Clerks***
43-4041.02	Credit Checkers***	33-9032.00	Security Guards***
53-3031.00	Driver/Sales Workers		

JOB ZONE 2 — ENTERPRISING — SUPPORT

O*NET-SOC#	O*NET-SOC Title	O*NET-SOC#	O*NET-SOC Title
43-4051.01	Adjustment Clerks***	43-4141.00	New Accounts Clerks***
43-3011.00	Bill and Account Collectors***	43-4151.00	Order Clerks***
43-4021.00	Correspondence Clerks***	43-5081.04	Order Fillers, Wholesale and Retail Sales***
43-4051.02	Customer Service Representatives, Utilities***	41-2022.00	Parts Salespersons
39-3012.00	Gaming and Sports Book Writers and Runners	43-3051.00	Payroll and Timekeeping Clerks***
39-3011.00	Gaming Dealers	43-5061.00	Production, Planning, and Expediting Clerks***
43-4081.00	Hotel, Motel, and Resort Desk Clerks***	43-4181.02	Reservation and Transportation Ticket Agents***
43-4161.00	Human Resources Assistants, Except Payroll and Timekeeping***	41-2031.00	Retail Salespersons
43-9041.01	Insurance Claims Clerks***	43-6014.00	Secretaries, Except Legal, Medical, and Executive***
43-9041.02	Insurance Policy Processing Clerks***	43-3021.01	Statement Clerks***
43-4031.03	License Clerks***	13-2082.00	Tax Preparers***
43-4131.00	Loan Interviewers and Clerks***	23-2093.01	Title Searchers***
43-4031.02	Municipal Clerks***		

JOB ZONE 3 — ENTERPRISING — SUPPORT

O*NET-SOC#	O*NET-SOC Title	O*NET-SOC#	O*NET-SOC Title
43-4031.01	Court Clerks***	53-5021.02	Mates- Ship, Boat, and Barge***
13-1041.04	Government Property Inspectors and Investigators	43-6013.00	Medical Secretaries***
33-3021.05	Immigration and Customs Inspectors***	13-1071.02	Personnel Recruiters
43-6012.00	Legal Secretaries***	49-9096.00	Riggers***
13-1041.02	Licensing Examiners and Inspectors***	23-2093.02	Title Examiners and Abstractors***

* Occupation included based on its highest interest area and second highest work value.
** Occupation included based on its highest interest area and third highest work value.
*** Occupation included based on its second highest interest area and highest work value.

ENTERPRISING — SUPPORT (continued)

JOB ZONE 4 — ENTERPRISING — SUPPORT

O*NET-SOC#	O*NET-SOC Title	O*NET-SOC#	O*NET-SOC Title
13-1031.01	Claims Examiners, Property and Casualty Insurance***	13-2053.00	Insurance Underwriters***
		13-2071.00	Loan Counselors
13-2041.00	Credit Analysts***	13-2072.00	Loan Officers
13-1041.03	Equal Opportunity Representatives and Officers***	53-6051.02	Public Transportation Inspectors
43-6011.00	Executive Secretaries and Administrative Assistants***	53-4031.00	Railroad Conductors and Yardmasters***
		13-2081.00	Tax Examiners, Collectors, and Revenue Agents***

JOB ZONE 5 — ENTERPRISING — SUPPORT

(No occupations for this combination in this job zone. To find occupations, look at other job zones in this combination or refer to the Interest and Work Value Master Lists.)

---

* Occupation included based on its highest interest area and second highest work value.
** Occupation included based on its highest interest area and third highest work value.
*** Occupation included based on its second highest interest area and highest work value.

ENTERPRISING — WORKING CONDITIONS

JOB ZONE 1 — ENTERPRISING — WORKING CONDITIONS

O*NET-SOC#	O*NET-SOC Title	O*NET-SOC#	O*NET-SOC Title
41-9091.00	Door-To-Door Sales Workers, News and Street Vendors, and Related Workers	41-9041.00	Telemarketers

(To find more occupations, look at other job zones in this combination or refer to the Interest and Work Value Master Lists.)

JOB ZONE 2 — ENTERPRISING — WORKING CONDITIONS

O*NET-SOC#	O*NET-SOC Title	O*NET-SOC#	O*NET-SOC Title
43-3021.02	Billing, Cost, and Rate Clerks***	43-4011.00	Brokerage Clerks***
43-3031.00	Bookkeeping, Accounting, and Auditing Clerks***	41-4011.03	Sales Representatives, Electrical/Electronic*

(To find more occupations, look at other job zones in this combination or refer to the Interest and Work Value Master Lists.)

JOB ZONE 3 — ENTERPRISING — WORKING CONDITIONS

O*NET-SOC#	O*NET-SOC Title
43-6012.00	Legal Secretaries***

(To find more occupations, look at other job zones in this combination or refer to the Interest and Work Value Master Lists.)

JOB ZONE 4 — ENTERPRISING — WORKING CONDITIONS

O*NET-SOC#	O*NET-SOC Title	O*NET-SOC#	O*NET-SOC Title
13-2011.01	Accountants***	13-2061.00	Financial Examiners
13-2021.01	Assessors***	23-2092.00	Law Clerks
13-2011.02	Auditors***	23-2011.00	Paralegals and Legal Assistants
13-2031.00	Budget Analysts***	11-9131.00	Postmasters and Mail Superintendents
13-1051.00	Cost Estimators***	11-3061.00	Purchasing Managers

JOB ZONE 5 — ENTERPRISING — WORKING CONDITIONS

O*NET-SOC#	O*NET-SOC Title	O*NET-SOC#	O*NET-SOC Title
23-1021.00	Administrative Law Judges, Adjudicators, and Hearing Officers*	11-1011.02	Private Sector Executives**
23-1022.00	Arbitrators, Mediators, and Conciliators*	11-3031.01	Treasurers, Controllers, and Chief Financial Officers*
23-1023.00	Judges, Magistrate Judges, and Magistrates**		

(To find more occupations, look at other job zones in this combination or refer to the Interest and Work Value Master Lists.)

* Occupation included based on its highest interest area and second highest work value.
** Occupation included based on its highest interest area and third highest work value.
*** Occupation included based on its second highest interest area and highest work value.

CONVENTIONAL

CONVENTIONAL — ACHIEVEMENT

JOB ZONE 1 — CONVENTIONAL — ACHIEVEMENT

(No occupations for this combination in this job zone. To find occupations, look at other job zones in this combination or refer to the Interest and Work Value Master Lists.)

JOB ZONE 2 — CONVENTIONAL — ACHIEVEMENT

O*NET-SOC#	O*NET-SOC Title	O*NET-SOC#	O*NET-SOC Title
49-3023.02	Automotive Specialty Technicians***	33-2022.00	Forest Fire Inspectors and Prevention Specialists***
47-2031.03	Carpenter Assemblers and Repairers***	47-2044.00	Tile and Marble Setters***
51-6092.00	Fabric and Apparel Patternmakers***	51-2093.00	Timing Device Assemblers, Adjusters, and
33-2021.01	Fire Inspectors		Calibrators***

JOB ZONE 3 — CONVENTIONAL — ACHIEVEMENT

O*NET-SOC#	O*NET-SOC Title	O*NET-SOC#	O*NET-SOC Title
49-3011.03	Aircraft Body and Bonded Structure Repairers***	39-1021.00	First-Line Supervisors/Managers of Personal Service
49-3021.00	Automotive Body and Related Repairers***		Workers***
49-3023.01	Automotive Master Mechanics***	17-3026.00	Industrial Engineering Technicians***
49-3031.00	Bus and Truck Mechanics and Diesel Engine	17-3031.02	Mapping Technicians
	Specialists***	49-3053.00	Outdoor Power Equipment and Other Small
17-3011.02	Civil Drafters***		Engine Mechanics***
13-1072.00	Compensation, Benefits, and Job Analysis	27-4013.00	Radio Operators***
	Specialists***	49-3043.00	Rail Car Repairers***
17-3012.01	Electronic Drafters***	47-2031.02	Rough Carpenters***
13-1041.01	Environmental Compliance Inspectors***	51-9071.02	Silversmiths***

---

* Occupation included based on its highest interest area and second highest work value.
** Occupation included based on its highest interest area and third highest work value.
*** Occupation included based on its second highest interest area and highest work value.

CONVENTIONAL — ACHIEVEMENT (continued)

JOB ZONE 4 — CONVENTIONAL — ACHIEVEMENT

O*NET-SOC#	O*NET-SOC Title	O*NET-SOC#	O*NET-SOC Title
53-2021.00	Air Traffic Controllers	11-2021.00	Marketing Managers***
47-2031.05	Boat Builders and Shipwrights***	17-3013.00	Mechanical Drafters***
17-1021.00	Cartographers and Photogrammetrists	51-4061.00	Model Makers, Metal and Plastic***
15-1041.00	Computer Support Specialists***	51-7031.00	Model Makers, Wood***
17-3012.02	Electrical Drafters	29-2081.00	Opticians, Dispensing***
11-3031.02	Financial Managers, Branch or Department***	51-7032.00	Patternmakers, Wood***
19-4092.00	Forensic Science Technicians***	29-1051.00	Pharmacists***
51-9195.04	Glass Blowers, Molders, Benders, and Finishers***	13-1023.00	Purchasing Agents, Except Wholesale, Retail, and Farm Products***
11-1011.01	Government Service Executives***		
13-1111.00	Management Analysts***	15-2041.00	Statisticians***

JOB ZONE 5 — CONVENTIONAL — ACHIEVEMENT

O*NET-SOC#	O*NET-SOC Title	O*NET-SOC#	O*NET-SOC Title
25-4011.00	Archivists***	15-2021.00	Mathematicians***
25-1021.00	Computer Science Teachers, Postsecondary***	11-3031.01	Treasurers, Controllers, and Chief Financial Officers***
23-1011.00	Lawyers***		

(To find more occupations, look at other job zones in this combination or refer to the Interest and Work Value Master Lists.)

---

* Occupation included based on its highest interest area and second highest work value.
** Occupation included based on its highest interest area and third highest work value.
*** Occupation included based on its second highest interest area and highest work value.

CONVENTIONAL — INDEPENDENCE

JOB ZONE 1 — CONVENTIONAL — INDEPENDENCE

(No occupations for this combination in this job zone. To find occupations, look at other job zones in this combination or refer to the Interest and Work Value Master Lists.)

JOB ZONE 2 — CONVENTIONAL — INDEPENDENCE

(No occupations for this combination in this job zone. To find occupations, look at other job zones in this combination or refer to the Interest and Work Value Master Lists.)

JOB ZONE 3 — CONVENTIONAL — INDEPENDENCE

O*NET-SOC#	O*NET-SOC Title	O*NET-SOC#	O*NET-SOC Title
15-1051.00	Computer Systems Analysts***	41-1011.00	First-Line Supervisors/Managers of Retail Sales Workers***
47-4011.00	Construction and Building Inspectors		
43-1011.02	First-Line Supervisors, Administrative Support***	11-9071.00	Gaming Managers***
53-1021.00	First-Line Supervisors/Managers of Helpers, Laborers, and Material Movers, Hand***	39-1011.00	Gaming Supervisors***
		11-9081.00	Lodging Managers***
41-1012.00	First-Line Supervisors/Managers of Non-Retail Sales Workers***	51-5022.07	Platemakers***
		41-3031.02	Sales Agents, Financial Services***
39-1021.00	First-Line Supervisors/Managers of Personal Service Workers***	51-9071.02	Silversmiths***
		13-1022.00	Wholesale and Retail Buyers, Except Farm Products***

JOB ZONE 4 — CONVENTIONAL — INDEPENDENCE

O*NET-SOC#	O*NET-SOC Title	O*NET-SOC#	O*NET-SOC Title
11-3011.00	Administrative Services Managers***	11-9141.00	Property, Real Estate, and Community Association Managers***
13-2021.02	Appraisers, Real Estate***		
13-1041.06	Coroners***	13-1021.00	Purchasing Agents and Buyers, Farm Products***
15-1061.00	Database Administrators***	41-3031.01	Sales Agents, Securities and Commodities***
11-9051.00	Food Service Managers***	11-2022.00	Sales Managers***
11-1011.01	Government Service Executives***	11-3071.02	Storage and Distribution Managers***
11-3051.00	Industrial Production Managers***	51-5022.06	Strippers***
13-1121.00	Meeting and Convention Planners***	11-3071.01	Transportation Managers***
15-2031.00	Operations Research Analysts***		

JOB ZONE 5 — CONVENTIONAL — INDEPENDENCE

O*NET-SOC#	O*NET-SOC Title	O*NET-SOC#	O*NET-SOC Title
11-3021.00	Computer and Information Systems Managers***	11-1011.02	Private Sector Executives***
13-2051.00	Financial Analysts***		

(To find more occupations, look at other job zones in this combination or refer to the Interest and Work Value Master Lists.)

---

* Occupation included based on its highest interest area and second highest work value.
** Occupation included based on its highest interest area and third highest work value.
*** Occupation included based on its second highest interest area and highest work value.

CONVENTIONAL — RECOGNITION

JOB ZONE 1 — CONVENTIONAL — RECOGNITION

(No occupations for this combination in this job zone. To find occupations, look at other job zones in this combination or refer to the Interest and Work Value Master Lists.)

JOB ZONE 2 — CONVENTIONAL — RECOGNITION

(No occupations for this combination in this job zone. To find occupations, look at other job zones in this combination or refer to the Interest and Work Value Master Lists.)

JOB ZONE 3 — CONVENTIONAL — RECOGNITION

(No occupations for this combination in this job zone. To find occupations, look at other job zones in this combination or refer to the Interest and Work Value Master Lists.)

JOB ZONE 4 — CONVENTIONAL — RECOGNITION

O*NET-SOC#	O*NET-SOC Title
53-2021.00	Air Traffic Controllers**

(To find more occupations, look at the Interest and Work Value Master Lists.)

JOB ZONE 5 — CONVENTIONAL — RECOGNITION

(No occupations for this combination in this job zone. To find occupations, look at other job zones in this combination or refer to the Interest and Work Value Master Lists.)

---

* Occupation included based on its highest interest area and second highest work value.
** Occupation included based on its highest interest area and third highest work value.
*** Occupation included based on its second highest interest area and highest work value.

CONVENTIONAL — RELATIONSHIPS

JOB ZONE 1 — CONVENTIONAL — RELATIONSHIPS

O*NET-SOC#	O*NET-SOC Title	O*NET-SOC#	O*NET-SOC Title
39-3091.00	Amusement and Recreation Attendants***	49-9098.00	Helpers—Installation, Maintenance, and Repair Workers***
41-2021.00	Counter and Rental Clerks		
43-5021.00	Couriers and Messengers***	47-3014.00	Helpers—Painters, Paperhangers, Plasterers, and Stucco Masons***
35-9021.00	Dishwashers***		
35-2021.00	Food Preparation Workers***	37-2012.00	Maids and Housekeeping Cleaners***
47-3011.00	Helpers—Brickmasons, Blockmasons, Stonemasons, and Tile and Marble Setters***	43-9061.00	Office Clerks, General
		51-6011.01	Spotters, Dry Cleaning***
47-3012.00	Helpers—Carpenters***	39-3031.00	Ushers, Lobby Attendants, and Ticket Takers***

JOB ZONE 2 — CONVENTIONAL — RELATIONSHIPS

O*NET-SOC#	O*NET-SOC Title	O*NET-SOC#	O*NET-SOC Title
49-3091.00	Bicycle Repairers***	29-2052.00	Pharmacy Technicians
35-2011.00	Cooks, Fast Food***	51-6021.01	Pressers, Delicate Fabrics***
35-2012.00	Cooks, Institution and Cafeteria***	21-1093.00	Social and Human Service Assistants***
47-3015.00	Helpers—Pipelayers, Plumbers, Pipefitters, and Steamfitters***	43-3071.00	Tellers
		43-4181.01	Travel Clerks
43-4081.00	Hotel, Motel, and Resort Desk Clerks	43-4061.02	Welfare Eligibility Workers and Interviewers***
25-4031.00	Library Technicians		

JOB ZONE 3 — CONVENTIONAL — RELATIONSHIPS

O*NET-SOC#	O*NET-SOC Title	O*NET-SOC#	O*NET-SOC Title
29-2021.00	Dental Hygienists***	39-9041.00	Residential Advisors***
31-9092.00	Medical Assistants***	25-9041.00	Teacher Assistants***
29-2071.00	Medical Records and Health Information Technicians		

(To find more occupations, look at other job zones in this combination or refer to the Interest and Work Value Master Lists.)

JOB ZONE 4 — CONVENTIONAL — RELATIONSHIPS

O*NET-SOC#	O*NET-SOC Title	O*NET-SOC#	O*NET-SOC Title
27-4011.00	Audio and Video Equipment Technicians	25-4021.00	Librarians***
25-9011.00	Audio-Visual Collections Specialists	47-2161.00	Plasterers and Stucco Masons***
39-4011.00	Embalmers***	29-2034.02	Radiologic Technicians***
37-1011.01	Housekeeping Supervisors***		

JOB ZONE 5 — CONVENTIONAL — RELATIONSHIPS

(No occupations for this combination in this job zone. To find occupations, look at other job zones in this combination or refer to the Interest and Work Value Master Lists.)

---

* Occupation included based on its highest interest area and second highest work value.
** Occupation included based on its highest interest area and third highest work value.
*** Occupation included based on its second highest interest area and highest work value.

CONVENTIONAL

CONVENTIONAL — SUPPORT

JOB ZONE 1 — CONVENTIONAL — SUPPORT

O*NET-SOC#	O*NET-SOC Title	O*NET-SOC#	O*NET-SOC Title
43-3021.03	Billing, Posting, and Calculating Machine Operators	43-5081.02	Marking Clerks
41-2011.00	Cashiers	43-5041.00	Meter Readers, Utilities
43-2021.02	Central Office Operators	43-9061.00	Office Clerks, General
43-4041.01	Credit Authorizers	33-3041.00	Parking Enforcement Workers
43-4041.02	Credit Checkers	43-5052.00	Postal Service Mail Carriers
43-2021.01	Directory Assistance Operators	43-3061.00	Procurement Clerks
43-9071.01	Duplicating Machine Operators	43-4171.00	Receptionists and Information Clerks
43-4071.00	File Clerks	43-5071.00	Shipping, Receiving, and Traffic Clerks
43-4111.00	Interviewers, Except Eligibility and Loan	43-2011.00	Switchboard Operators, Including Answering Service
43-4121.00	Library Assistants, Clerical		
43-9051.02	Mail Clerks, Except Mail Machine Operators and Postal Service	43-5111.00	Weighers, Measurers, Checkers, and Samplers, Recordkeeping

JOB ZONE 2 — CONVENTIONAL — SUPPORT

O*NET-SOC#	O*NET-SOC Title	O*NET-SOC#	O*NET-SOC Title
43-4051.01	Adjustment Clerks	43-4141.00	New Accounts Clerks
43-3011.00	Bill and Account Collectors	43-4151.00	Order Clerks
43-5011.00	Cargo and Freight Agents	43-5081.04	Order Fillers, Wholesale and Retail Sales
43-4061.01	Claims Takers, Unemployment Benefits	43-3051.00	Payroll and Timekeeping Clerks
43-4021.00	Correspondence Clerks	43-5051.00	Postal Service Clerks
43-4051.02	Customer Service Representatives, Utilities	43-5061.00	Production, Planning, and Expediting Clerks
43-9021.00	Data Entry Keyers	43-9081.00	Proofreaders and Copy Markers
43-5032.00	Dispatchers, Except Police, Fire, and Ambulance	43-4181.02	Reservation and Transportation Ticket Agents
53-6051.06	Freight Inspectors	43-6014.00	Secretaries, Except Legal, Medical, and Executive
43-4081.00	Hotel, Motel, and Resort Desk Clerks	43-3021.01	Statement Clerks
43-4161.00	Human Resources Assistants, Except Payroll and Timekeeping	43-5081.03	Stock Clerks- Stockroom, Warehouse, or Storage Yard
43-9041.01	Insurance Claims Clerks	13-2082.00	Tax Preparers
43-9041.02	Insurance Policy Processing Clerks	23-2093.01	Title Searchers
43-4031.03	License Clerks	43-4181.01	Travel Clerks
43-4131.00	Loan Interviewers and Clerks	43-9022.00	Word Processors and Typists
43-4031.02	Municipal Clerks		

JOB ZONE 3 — CONVENTIONAL — SUPPORT

O*NET-SOC#	O*NET-SOC Title	O*NET-SOC#	O*NET-SOC Title
49-2011.01	Automatic Teller Machine Servicers***	51-4193.01	Electrolytic Plating and Coating Machine Setters and Set-Up Operators, Metal and Plastic***
51-4072.05	Casting Machine Set-Up Operators***		
19-4061.01	City Planning Aides	49-2096.00	Electronic Equipment Installers and Repairers, Motor Vehicles***
51-4081.01	Combination Machine Tool Setters and Set-Up Operators, Metal and Plastic***	51-5023.07	Embossing Machine Set-Up Operators***
49-2022.03	Communication Equipment Mechanics, Installers, and Repairers***	51-2031.00	Engine and Other Machine Assemblers***
		51-8092.02	Gas Distribution Plant Operators***
43-9011.00	Computer Operators	51-8093.03	Gaugers***
43-4031.00	Court Clerks	19-4041.01	Geological Data Technicians***
51-2022.00	Electrical and Electronic Equipment Assemblers***	13-1041.04	Government Property Inspectors and Investigators***
51-9061.04	Electrical and Electronic Inspectors and Testers***		
49-2093.00	Electrical and Electronics Installers and Repairers, Transportation Equipment***	51-4033.01	Grinding, Honing, Lapping, and Deburring Machine Set-Up Operators***

* Occupation included based on its highest interest area and second highest work value.
** Occupation included based on its highest interest area and third highest work value.
*** Occupation included based on its second highest interest area and highest work value.

CONVENTIONAL — SUPPORT (continued)

JOB ZONE 3 — CONVENTIONAL — SUPPORT (CONTINUED)

O*NET-SOC#	O*NET-SOC Title	O*NET-SOC#	O*NET-SOC Title
51-4191.01	Heating Equipment Setters and Set-Up Operators, Metal and Plastic***	51-9061.03	Precision Devices Inspectors and Testers***
33-3021.05	Immigration and Customs Inspectors	51-9195.01	Precision Mold and Pattern Casters, except Nonferrous Metals***
51-4034.00	Lathe and Turning Machine Tool Setters, Operators, and Tenders, Metal and Plastic***	21-1092.00	Probation Officers and Correctional Treatment Specialists***
51-4192.00	Lay-Out Workers, Metal and Plastic***	47-2171.00	Reinforcing Iron and Rebar Workers***
43-6012.00	Legal Secretaries	47-5012.00	Rotary Drill Operators, Oil and Gas***
51-5023.03	Letterpress Setters and Set-Up Operators***	51-5023.06	Screen Printing Machine Setters and Set-Up Operators***
13-1041.02	Licensing Examiners and Inspectors	51-8021.02	Stationary Engineers***
53-4012.00	Locomotive Firers***	51-6062.00	Textile Cutting Machine Setters, Operators, and Tenders***
49-9042.00	Maintenance and Repair Workers, General***	51-6063.00	Textile Knitting and Weaving Machine Setters, Operators, and Tenders***
51-9061.01	Materials Inspectors***	51-6064.00	Textile Winding, Twisting, and Drawing Out Machine Setters, Operators, and Tenders***
43-6013.00	Medical Secretaries	23-2093.02	Title Examiners and Abstractors
51-4035.00	Milling and Planing Machine Setters, Operators, and Tenders, Metal and Plastic***	51-4194.00	Tool Grinders, Filers, and Sharpeners***
51-4193.03	Nonelectrolytic Plating and Coating Machine Setters and Set-Up Operators, Metal and Plastic***	49-9012.02	Valve and Regulator Repairers***
49-2011.03	Office Machine and Cash Register Servicers***	51-4122.01	Welding Machine Setters and Set-Up Operators***
51-8093.01	Petroleum Pump System Operators***		
33-3021.02	Police Identification and Records Officers		

JOB ZONE 4 — CONVENTIONAL — SUPPORT

O*NET-SOC#	O*NET-SOC Title	O*NET-SOC#	O*NET-SOC Title
17-3023.02	Calibration and Instrumentation Technicians***	51-9083.02	Optical Instrument Assemblers***
13-1031.01	Claims Examiners, Property and Casualty Insurance	51-4062.00	Patternmakers, Metal and Plastic***
13-2041.00	Credit Analysts	51-8012.00	Power Distributors and Dispatchers***
49-9051.00	Electrical Power-Line Installers and Repairers***	51-8013.01	Power Generating Plant Operators, Except Auxiliary Equipment Operators***
51-5023.08	Engraver Set-Up Operators***	51-9195.02	Precision Pattern and Die Casters, Nonferrous Metals***
43-6011.00	Executive Secretaries and Administrative Assistants	13-1041.05	Pressure Vessel Inspectors***
51-2041.02	Fitters, Structural Metal- Precision***	53-6051.02	Public Transportation Inspectors***
53-7071.02	Gas Compressor Operators***	49-9021.02	Refrigeration Mechanics***
51-5022.01	Hand Compositors and Typesetters***	49-9097.00	Signal and Track Switch Repairers***
13-1032.00	Insurance Appraisers, Auto Damage	49-2022.05	Station Installers and Repairers, Telephone***
13-2053.00	Insurance Underwriters	17-3031.01	Surveying Technicians***
53-4011.00	Locomotive Engineers***	13-2081.00	Tax Examiners, Collectors, and Revenue Agents
51-9061.02	Mechanical Inspectors***	51-4111.00	Tool and Die Makers***
51-2041.01	Metal Fabricators, Structural Metal Products***	53-7073.00	Wellhead Pumpers***
51-8011.00	Nuclear Power Reactor Operators***		

JOB ZONE 5 — CONVENTIONAL — SUPPORT

O*NET-SOC#	O*NET-SOC Title	O*NET-SOC#	O*NET-SOC Title
51-5022.10	Electrotypers and Stereotypers***	51-5022.11	Plate Finishers***
53-6051.03	Marine Cargo Inspectors		
51-5023.02	Offset Lithographic Press Setters and Set-Up Operators***		

(To find more occupations, look at other job zones in this combination or refer to the Interest and Work Value Master Lists.)

---

* Occupation included based on its highest interest area and second highest work value.
** Occupation included based on its highest interest area and third highest work value.
*** Occupation included based on its second highest interest area and highest work value.

CONVENTIONAL — WORKING CONDITIONS

JOB ZONE 1 — CONVENTIONAL — WORKING CONDITIONS

O*NET-SOC#	O*NET-SOC Title	O*NET-SOC#	O*NET-SOC Title
43-3021.03	Billing, Posting, and Calculating Machine Operators*	43-5052.00	Postal Service Mail Carriers*
		43-3061.00	Procurement Clerks*
43-4041.01	Credit Authorizers*	43-2011.00	Switchboard Operators, Including Answering Service*
43-4041.02	Credit Checkers*		
43-9051.02	Mail Clerks, Except Mail Machine Operators and Postal Service*		

JOB ZONE 2 — CONVENTIONAL — WORKING CONDITIONS

O*NET-SOC#	O*NET-SOC Title	O*NET-SOC#	O*NET-SOC Title
43-3021.02	Billing, Cost, and Rate Clerks	43-3051.00	Payroll and Timekeeping Clerks*
43-3031.00	Bookkeeping, Accounting, and Auditing Clerks	29-2052.00	Pharmacy Technicians*
43-4011.00	Brokerage Clerks	43-9081.00	Proofreaders and Copy Markers*
43-4161.00	Human Resources Assistants, Except Payroll and Timekeeping*	43-6014.00	Secretaries, Except Legal, Medical, and Executive*
		43-9111.00	Statistical Assistants
43-4031.02	Municipal Clerks*	23-2093.01	Title Searchers*

JOB ZONE 3 — CONVENTIONAL — WORKING CONDITIONS

O*NET-SOC#	O*NET-SOC Title	O*NET-SOC#	O*NET-SOC Title
51-9071.04	Bench Workers, Jewelry***	51-4012.00	Numerical Tool and Process Control Programmers***
49-2092.02	Electric Motor and Switch Assemblers and Repairers***	51-9131.02	Photographic Reproduction Technicians***
49-2097.00	Electronic Home Entertainment Equipment Installers and Repairers***	51-9083.01	Precision Lens Grinders and Polishers***
		49-2021.00	Radio Mechanics***
43-6012.00	Legal Secretaries	51-6052.01	Shop and Alteration Tailors***
49-9094.00	Locksmiths and Safe Repairers***	49-9064.00	Watch Repairers***
29-2071.00	Medical Records and Health Information Technicians		

JOB ZONE 4 — CONVENTIONAL — WORKING CONDITIONS

O*NET-SOC#	O*NET-SOC Title	O*NET-SOC#	O*NET-SOC Title
13-2011.01	Accountants	49-9021.01	Heating and Air Conditioning Mechanics***
13-2021.01	Assessors	23-2092.00	Law Clerks***
13-2011.02	Auditors	23-2011.00	Paralegals and Legal Assistants***
13-2031.00	Budget Analysts	51-5022.02	Paste-Up Workers***
13-1051.00	Cost Estimators	11-9131.00	Postmasters and Mail Superintendents***
49-2011.00	Data Processing Equipment Repairers***	11-3061.00	Purchasing Managers***
51-5022.09	Electronic Masking System Operators***	51-5022.05	Scanner Operators***
13-2061.00	Financial Examiners***		

* Occupation included based on its highest interest area and second highest work value.
** Occupation included based on its highest interest area and third highest work value.
*** Occupation included based on its second highest interest area and highest work value.

CONVENTIONAL — WORKING CONDITIONS (continued)

JOB ZONE 5 — CONVENTIONAL — WORKING CONDITIONS

O*NET-SOC#	O*NET-SOC Title	O*NET-SOC#	O*NET-SOC Title
15-2011.00	Actuaries	51-5021.00	Job Printers***
51-5022.08	Dot Etchers***	53-6051.03	Marine Cargo Inspectors*

(To find more occupations, look at other job zones in this combination or refer to the Interest and Work Value Master Lists.)

* Occupation included based on its highest interest area and second highest work value.
** Occupation included based on its highest interest area and third highest work value.
*** Occupation included based on its second highest interest area and highest work value.

Appendix C

Career-Related Internet and World Wide Web Sites

Career Research

www.wetfeet.com

www.acinet.org

www.princetonreview.com

Company Research

www.wetfeet.com

www.hoovers.com

Finding Jobs

Sites that allow you to setup search agents and store your resume:

www.careerbuilder.com

www.monster.com

www.hotjobs.com

Site that allows you to search more than one site at a time:

www.alljobsearch.com

Niche sites

Federal/State

www.federaljobsearch.com

www.statejobs.com

Nonprofit/Social Services

http://philanthropy.com/jobs

Minorities

www.imdiversity.com

Women

www.ivillage.com/work

www.careerwomen.com

Baby Boomers

www.aarp.org/working_options

Part-Time/Students/Entry-Level

www.groovejob.com

Executives

www.careerjournal.com

www.sixfigurejobs.com

www.execunet.com

General Sites

www.directemployers.com

www.brassring.com

www.flipdog.com

Career Advice

www.monster.com
www.damngood.com
www.wetfeet.com
www.jobstar.org
www.jobhuntersbible.com
www.rileyguide.com
www.careerperfect.com
www.net-temps.com
www.job-hunt.org
www.employmentzone.org
http://online.onetcenter.org

Salary Information

www.salary.com
www.acinet.org
www.monster.com

Networking Information

www.vistaprints.com (business cards)
Check your local Chamber of Commerce Web site.

General WWW Searches

www.google.com
www.ask.com
www.yahoo.com

Other Sites

Download software to improve typing speed and accuracy:
www.typingmaster.com

Internet Learning:
www.learnthenet.com
http://whatis.com
www.pcwebopedia.com

Internet Safety and Privacy
http://resume.monster.com/articles/personalinfo
http://www.job-hunt.org/privacy.shtml

Internet Don'ts
www.job-hunt.org
www.resumania.com

Volunteer
www.volunteermatch.org

Appendix D

⌐∾⌐

People Resources for
Career Decision-Making Assistance

Career Counselors
- Assist with many aspects of your career planning and development
- Help you understand your values, interests, skills, and personal situation
- Provide information about occupations, employers, and your labor market
- Suggest activities that will help you identify new career options
- Help you refine your employability skills such as writing resumes, identifying prospective employers, and interviewing
- May serve as valuable referral sources

The National Career Development Association can help you identify a career counselor in your area. Call toll free (866) FOR NCDA.

Career Resource Centers
- Usually staffed by professional counselors
- Often have print, audio, video, and computer resources available
- Assist with career concerns through vocational assessment, providing career information, and evaluating employability skills and career issues specific to a certain population
- Usually in colleges and universities, though some are community based
- State-sponsored vocational education centers are equipped to address special needs in adults

Chambers of Commerce
If you are seeking information about employers in a certain geographic area, a good place to start is with the appropriate Chamber of Commerce.

Employment Lawyers
Sometimes, individuals need assistance with evaluating sensitive workplace issues such as discrimination, wrongful termination, retaliation, and sexual harassment – a lawyer specializing in employment law can help.

Job Clubs
Belonging to a group of people who share your goal of finding jobs has several advantages. Members of job clubs are usually people with diverse backgrounds, skills, and interests, who can offer one another leads on various job openings, developing a job campaign strategy, and support. Many of the people resources listed in this appendix can refer you to local job clubs.

Labor Unions
You can obtain current information about a specific occupation, organization, or industry by contacting the appropriate labor union.

Personal Network
This is composed of the following potential resources for developing your career:
- Friends
- Relatives

- Neighbors
- Coworkers
- Faith-based and social organizations
- Former teachers and employers
- Customers and competitors

Using your personal network is limited only by your level of resourcefulness and creativity. You can use it to identify training or job opportunities, to get an inside view of an organization, and to obtain firsthand information and advice from someone who has attained career goals to which you aspire.

Personnel Departments

The following information can usually be obtained through an organization's personnel department:

- Personnel policy
- Human resources planning
- Organizational goals
- Recruiting literature
- Annual reports from public organizations

Professional Associations

Besides making contacts with people who share your professional interests, being active in a professional association, either locally or nationally, offers many career-related benefits. Most professional associations publish journals and newsletters that are excellent sources of career information ranging from salary surveys and trends in an industry to classified advertisements of job openings. Some professional associations sponsor workshops and conventions that address the profession's state-of-the-art issues and developments. Many of these conventions also offer placement assistance to interested individuals.

Recruiters

Most large organizations employ in-house search consultants who are responsible for finding qualified candidates to fill its positions. Recruiters often go to college campuses, professional association conventions and meetings, and job fairs to find and interview prospective employees.

Reference Librarian

Available in most libraries, they can help you find a diversity of rich career information quickly.

Resume Preparer

Your resume, often your first contact with your prospective employer, is an important job-finding tool. Resume preparers can help develop your resume by showing you samples of other resumes, helping you articulate your background, and suggesting a format to present your credentials. They can also help with your resume's physical production.

Search Consultants

These people usually work for a firm retained by an employer to find, screen, and refer qualified candidates for various jobs. They often specialize in an industry or occupational field. If you choose to use an executive search consultant's services, be sure that you first understand and agree with the method of payment.

Department of Labor

Labor market statistics of all sorts, including wage earnings by geographic areas, demographic groups, and occupational areas, are compiled by your state's Department of Labor. You can obtain this information on request or by consulting public documents in most large libraries.

Department of Professional Regulation

You can learn about the requirements necessary to practice various regulated professions within your state by contacting the Department of Professional Regulation. Some states may use titles such as Department of Business and Professional Regulation, Financial and Professional Regulation, or Professional and Occupational Regulation, to name a few.

State Employment Service

While each state's employment services vary, they usually provide listings of local and state job openings and general information on state and federal employment. Some state employment services also offer aptitude testing, local labor-market information, career counseling, and assistance in settling grievances concerning unfair treatment by an employer.

Vocational Rehabilitation Programs

People with physical or mental disabilities can obtain various services designed to prepare them for employment and to help them get a job through their participation in a vocational rehabilitation program. In accordance with the Americans with Disabilities Act, vocational rehabilitation counselors can also help to identify job accommodations to help individuals with disabilities work around their limitations.

Work Evaluation Centers

Located in private as well as nonprofit organizations, work evaluation centers usually contain several simulated work stations designed to assess individuals' skills in performing different tasks. Some centers also offer career guidance services.

Appendix E

Bibliography of
Print Resources

Brown, D. (2002). Introduction to theories of career development and choice. In D. Brown (Ed.), *Career Choice and Development* (4th ed., pp. 3-23). San Francisco: Jossey-Bass.

Enelow, Wendy S., and Shelly Goldman. *Insider's Guide to Finding a Job: Expert Advice from America's Top Employers and Recruiters.* Indianapolis: JIST Works, 2004. ISBN: 1-59357-077-5

Farley, Janet I. *Military-to-Civilian Career Transition Guide: The Essential Job Search Handbook For Service Members.* Indianapolis: JIST Publishing, 2004. ISBN 1-59357-091-0

Farr, J. Michael. *Getting the Job You Really Want,* 4th ed. Indianapolis: JIST Works, 2002. ISBN: 1-56370-803-5

Farr, J. Michael, and LaVerne L. Ludden. *300 Best Jobs Without a Four-year Degree.* Indianapolis: JIST Works, 2003. ISBN: 1-56370-861-2

Geary, Gail. *Over-40 Job Search Guide: 10 Strategies for Making Your Age an Advantage in Your Career.* Indianapolis: JIST Publishing, 2004. ISBN: 1-59357-090-2

Gottfredson, G. D., & Holland, J. L. (1996) *The Dictionary of Holland Occupational Codes.* Odessa, FL: Psychological Assessment Resources.

Gottfredson, G. D. (1999). John L. Holland's contributions to vocational psychology: A review and evaluation. *Journal of Vocational Behavior,* 55, 15-40.

Harris-Bowlsbey, JoAnn, Dikel, Margaret R., and James P. Sampson, Jr. *The Internet: A Tool for Career Planning.* 2nd ed. Tulsa, OK: National Career Development Association, 2002. ISBN: 1-885333-10-2

Holland, J. L. (1973). *Making Vocational Choices: A Theory of Careers.* Englewood Cliffs, NJ: Prentice Hall.

Holland, J. L. (1997). *Making Vocational Choices: A Theory of Vocational Personalities and Work Environments.* Odessa, FL: Psychological Assessment Resources, Inc.

Kursmark, Louise M. *Sales and Marketing Resumes for $100,000 Careers.* 2nd ed. Indianapolis: JIST Publishing, 2004. ISBN: 1-59357-013-9

Muchinsky, P. M. (1999). Application of Holland's theory in industrial and organizational settings. *Journal of Vocational Behavior,* 55, 127-35.

Reardon, R. C., Sampson, J. P., Jr., & Lenz, J. G. (2000). Career assessment in a time of changing roles, relationships, and contexts. *Journal of Career Assessment,* 8, 351-359.

Ryan, Daniel J. *Job Search Handbook for People with Disabilities*. 2nd ed. Indianapolis: JIST Publishing, 2004. ISBN: 156370-989-9

Schlossberg, Nancy K. *Retire Smart, Retire Happy: Finding Your True Path in Life*. Washington, DC: American Psychological Association, 2003. ISBN: 1-59147-039-0

Tullier, L. Michelle. *Networking for Job Search and Career Success*. 2nd ed. Indianapolis: JIST Publishing, 2004. ISBN: 1-59357-067-8

U.S. Department of Labor. *Enhanced Occupational Outlook Handbook*, 5th ed. Edited by J. Michael Farr with Laurence Shatkin. Indianapolis: JIST Publishing, 2005. ISBN: 1-59357-031-7

U.S. Department of Labor. *Occupational Outlook Handbook*, 2004-2005. Indianapolis: JIST Publishing, Published annually. ISBN: 1-56370-987-2

Appendix F

Organizing Your Job Search

Information Interview Summary and Evaluation Sheet

Referred by: _____   Title: _____

Organization:_____   Date: _____

Contact:_____   Title: _____

Organization:_____   Phone: _____

Others met (names and titles):

_____   _____

_____   _____

Referrals (names and titles) for future interviews:

_____   _____

_____   _____

_____   _____

Overall meeting evaluation: _____

_____

_____

_____

Things done particularly well: _____

_____

Things that could be improved: _____

_____

Tough or unusual questions to practice before next meeting: _____

_____

_____

_____

Next steps:

Thank-you letter on:_____   Follow-up call on: _____

Presenting Your Accomplishments

To most employers, your accomplishments speak louder than descriptions of past job responsibilities. Think about your accomplishments using the following action terms:

- Consolidated . . .
- Documented . . .
- Structured . . .
- Supervised . . .
- Designed . . .
- Improved productivity by . . .
- Reduced turnover by . . .
- Recruited . . .
- Trained . . .
- Managed a $ _____ budget . . .
- Reduced time allocations by . . .
- Built . . .
- Revised organizational plans . . .
- Evaluated . . .
- Reduced customer complaints by . . .
- Enhanced community relations by . . .
- Improved product quality by . . .
- Set new goals . . .
- Organized . . .
- Eliminated obsolete . . .
- Planned . . .
- Repaired . . .
- Developed . . .
- Recovered . . .
- Created . . .
- Implemented . . .

Guidelines for Telephone Use

1. Organize your information before the call; a planning sheet is recommended. Have a resume and the following information in front of you:
    - Name of person you want to reach
    - Information you need
    - Key points you want to stress in opening statement
    - Results you plan to achieve

2. Practice for each call. Anticipate questions and objections that will end a conversation – particularly receptionists' questions, such as, "What is this in reference to?" Decide before the call how you will answer these questions. Among the most effective ways to get through a screening is to sound professional and confident. Citing referral sources may also help.

3. Try to sound confident and relaxed.

4. Avoid being interviewed on the phone. Your main goal is to secure a face-to-face meeting. An alternative is to have the person refer you to someone else.

5. Don't talk too long. Maintain a balance between listening and talking.

6. Take notes during the conversation and immediately afterward. Review them before the interview.

Job Interview Summary and Evaluation Sheet

Name: _____   Title: _____

Organization:_____   Phone: _____

Secretary:_____

Referral source: _____

Others met (names and titles):

_____   _____

_____   _____

Information about the position in question: _____

_____

_____

Things that could have gone better:_____

_____

_____

Tough or unusual questions to practice:_____

_____

_____

Overall impression: _____

_____

_____

Next steps:

Thank-you letter on:_____   Follow-up call on: _____

Daily Job Search Plan

Date:_____ Job targets:_____

Job campaign hours: from _____ to _____

Primary objectives for the day: _____

Telephone Calls or Letters

Person / Organization	Contact Info.	Objective	Result

Research Objectives

Sources	Objective	Result

Objective — Weekly Job Search Plan

Activity	Monday	Tuesday	Wednesday	Thursday	Friday	Saturday	Sunday
Planning							
Self-Exploration							
Targeting and Labor Market Research							
Phone Calls							
Writing Letters							
Non-Job Trips (Library, Interview, Research)							
Job Interviews							
Meetings with Third Parties							
Practice, Develop Job Skills							
Review, Respond to Ads							
Meet with Search Firms							

Research Objectives (continued)

Sources	Monday	Tuesday	Wednesday	Thursday	Friday	Saturday	Sunday
Career Counseling							
_____							
_____							
_____							
_____							
_____							
_____							
DAILY TOTALS							
WEEKLY TOTAL							

Comparison of Job Offers

How closely do the positions match my stated goals?

No match . . . 1 2 3 4 5 . . . Almost perfect match

	JOB A	JOB B
Organization's image/reputation	_____	_____
Industry direction	_____	_____
Organization culture	_____	_____
Work activities	_____	_____
Job functions	_____	_____
Growth potential	_____	_____
Career potential	_____	_____
Management style	_____	_____
Coworkers	_____	_____
Security factors	_____	_____
Compensation	_____	_____
Review process	_____	_____
Training	_____	_____
Challenge	_____	_____
Corporate structure	_____	_____
Level of responsibility	_____	_____
Title	_____	_____
Job resources	_____	_____
Facilities	_____	_____
Location	_____	_____
Travel requirement	_____	_____
Other factors	_____	_____
. . . .	_____	_____
. . . .	_____	_____